London Froebel Society

Essays on the Kindergarten

Being a Selection of Lectures read before the London Froebel Society

London Froebel Society

Essays on the Kindergarten
Being a Selection of Lectures read before the London Froebel Society

ISBN/EAN: 9783337130756

Printed in Europe, USA, Canada, Australia, Japan

Cover: Foto ©ninafisch / pixelio.de

More available books at **www.hansebooks.com**

ESSAYS
ON THE
KINDERGARTEN

BEING A SELECTION OF

Lectures Read before the London Froebel Society

SECOND  EDITION

LONDON
SWAN SONNENSCHEIN, LOWREY & CO.
PATERNOSTER SQUARE
1887

CONTENTS.

	PAGE
MADAME DE PORTUGALL's Synoptical Table . *Frons.*	
No. 1.—SHIRREFF, Progressive Development according to Fröbel's Principles	5
No. 2.—BUCKLAND, On Stories in the Kindergarten . . .	19
No. 3.—HOGGAN, Physical Education of Girls	36
No. 4.—BUCKLAND, The Happiness of Childhood . . .	60
No. 5.—HEERWART, Fröbel's Mutter und Kose-lieder . . .	81
No. 6.—SHIRREFF, Wasted Forces	99
No. 7.—SHIRREFF, The Kindergarten in Relation to Schools .	116
No. 8.—SHIRREFF, The Kindergarten in Relation to Family Life.	133

PROGRESSIVE DEVELOPMENT

ACCORDING TO

FRÖBEL'S PRINCIPLES OF EDUCATION.

By EMILY SHIRREFF.*

My purpose this evening is to draw your attention to the Synoptical Table that Madame de Portugall has constructed, to show the intimate connection between the kindergarten and all later studies. You see it here before you, enlarged, and also slightly simplified, in as far as some of the less important details have been omitted, to avoid overcrowding, so that it might be clearly seen from a distance. We must suppose this table to represent the whole period of life given to instruction, *i.e.*, kindergarten age, from three to seven; school time, from seven to eighteen; higher studies, from eighteen upwards, according to opportunities and the degree of knowledge aimed at. These different portions are marked out here. All the lower part, beginning from this central point, is devoted to the kindergarten. The school

---

* This paper was written for a lecture, delivered before the Froebel Society, and is printed in the form in which it was originally delivered.

occupies the space bounded below and above by the double horizontal lines, B and C, and all the space beyond this where the lines again converge to a point, represents the period of higher culture. The lines, either perpendicular or slightly inclined, that you see beginning in the kindergarten portion, and passing through the other sections, are intended to mark the connection of the lessons or play of one period with the studies of another; each later study being underlined with the same colour as that of the ascending line that leads up to it, and this we must bear in mind is intended to mark a real connection, for, as Madame de Portugall tells us in her pamphlet, "when I say '*lead up to them*,' I do not mean simply that the branches of later instruction follow upon them, but grow out of them, and that the kindergarten training begins upon the same lines of thought which are followed throughout. There is everywhere development, but not change." Madame de Portugall's purpose in constructing this table was just to bring this connection prominently forward. This conception of continuity is at the very root of Fröbel's system; but, like other principles, is too often neglected. While the mere exterior of the method grows in popular favour, I cannot do better, in order to point out its importance, than to quote, as Madame de Portugall has done in her short explanation of the table, a passage from Fröbel himself. "It is," he says, "of the highest importance, not only for the religious development of man, but for the expansion of all his faculties, that his education, starting from *one point*, should follow a progressive course, and should advance towards the goal uninterruptedly, without breaks or sudden changes. For nothing is more hurtful to the development of the individual than to consider any stage as detached or isolated from the rest. The periods of life known as childhood, youth, adolescence, manhood, old age, are but the links of one and the same chain, and, consequently, the little child, the youth, the man in his maturity, cannot be looked upon as different beings, strangers one to the other. Life, in all its various phases, presents one complex whole, of which it must be our care to consider the starting-point and the ultimate goal." "The bearing of these words," adds Madame de Portugall, "on all education is immense; yet the pedagogical principle they contain presents much difficulty, and, even now, attracts little attention. No earnest-minded man, or real educator, can overlook it; he knows its value, and how much depends on its practical application; but it is not recognized by the public."

Let us now turn to the table. It shows us the whole system of kindergarten gifts and occupations as resting upon three objects presenting three fundamental forms—the *ball*, the *cube*, and the *cylinder*. All three are contained in the *second gift*, as Fröbel calls his boxes of lesson toys. The ball, the uniform sphere, the cube with its straight lines and flat surfaces, the cylinder that partakes of both, presenting a rounded surface like the ball, and lines and flat surfaces like the cube. The cylinder is the first example Fröbel gives of the intermediate transition-forms connecting opposites, which he explains as the very ground-plan of nature, and on which his fundamental law of contrasts and connection of contrasts, the law of all harmonious development and creative industry, is based.

Madame de Portugall's table starts from the *ball* as the first fundamental form. It occupies the centre of the lowest part of the table. We see it at the root, so to speak, of the spreading branches we have to follow into their various ramifications. As belonging immediately to the ball, we have here *ball-games*, which are the first in which the baby class is led to take interest, and through the means of which are taught certain movements, single and combined, giving the first idea of time and rhythm. The difference between hard and soft balls, balls of different sizes and colour, etc., is also learned here. From these games there is an easy passage to gymnastic games, which are generally made to exemplify some little story or description, and which, being always accompanied with music, carry on the lesson of time and rhythm begun with the ball games, and are closely connected with that very important part of early kindergarten instruction, the art of *story-telling*.

Madame de Portugall places both languages and stories together, as belonging to the early series of exercises. We see, without need of explanation, how immediate is the connection between the child's first study of language and his first interest in stories. It will not be a grammatical study certainly. That will not come till long after, but a study of words and sentences, which the teacher will always make sure her little audience understands. New words, or new forms of expression, will often be purposely introduced into a narrative, and from these new words, names, probably, of things which the children are promised a sight of next day, or which they have seen but not noticed, a fresh tale may begin. For there are no set stories in the kindergarten, nor is it yet the time for fables, save of the most artless kind; the satire and worldly wisdom which underlie their apparent simplicity make them unfit for those who can as yet see a very small portion of the surface of things. The little narratives I speak of are just what the present object, or game, or child's question, suggests. The children, though generally eager to know, and prompt to feel, are ignorant of all, and the teacher knows so much of what surrounds their ignorance—at least we hope she does—that materials can never fail.

However, I have not undertaken to discourse here upon storytelling, but only to show how fitly stories are placed at the base of all studies connected with language, and how they all spring from exercises with that first fundamental form, the ball. We have already noticed that the earliest lesson upon colours will be given in connection with it; the only thing that remains to be noticed on this part of the table is modelling. The first childish attempt in this art is directed to model a ball; and though the child never produces a correct sphere, he comes nearer to rolling up his lump of clay into a ball than he would at this same stage arrive at producing any object of greater complexity, or requiring accurate lines. No one who has seen a child model his ball will doubt that this first exercise of manual productiveness affords him a degree of pleasure which may give a new vent to the material instinct of activity within him, while exercising his eye and fingers; and few who have not seen it, realize how soon from the ball he will make an orange, clearly distinguishing the difference of form; and thence an apple, or a pear, which again lead him eagerly to want stalks, and leaves, etc.: or the ball is hollowed to form a nest, into which little balls are carefully placed as eggs, and thence follows pleasant talk of birds and their haunts, the trees, the hedges, etc. A little reflection upon this will show us how justly Madame de Portugall carries up her section of modelling right through the period of school studies till it reaches sculpture and the fine arts generally. Not one in twenty, perhaps not one in a hundred, it may be, of these children will ever reach that stage; they may have no taste, no talent, no opportunity for it. Yet should they not, the first great object of all education has still been forwarded, by the drawing out of a natural aptitude, a possession prepared for after use if needed, for delight whenever used.

If we follow on the table the other lines that are carried up from the ball games to the division of school studies, we see in the intermediate portion, *reading*, and *writing*, and *knowledge of native place*. It requires no explanation to show why the former should be placed immediately following language and stories, and therefore be marked with the same coloured lines. If we interest children with stories, it is to excite that pleasure in knowledge, that interest in the life around them, which will later seek its own food in books; and it is evident that writing is only one branch of the study of language—written words are, in our state of civilization, only of secondary necessity to spoken words; and as soon as the child becomes apt in speech, he must be led to seek the art of tracing his words on paper. Reading and writing are taught, as you know, simultaneously in these schools; but not in the kindergarten proper. Fröbel had a dread of all the false notions, the half-understood words that children get hold of by early reading to themselves, and he knew also how short is the time we can command for that more important work of developing their faculties amid the phenomena of the visible world, before book-learning makes its inevitable and ever-growing claim upon the understanding and the memory. Thus you see on this table reading and writing are placed half-way between kindergarten games and school lessons. They are given over to the transition class which receives the child at seven years old to prepare him for the change from entirely concrete to partly abstract teaching; from that which appeals to the mind through the senses, and that which appeals to the understanding mostly or altogether. The knowledge of our native place, which occupies a parallel position on the table, is also derived, as we are shown by the colour of the lines, from language and stories, with the addition of gymnastic games. The connection of the latter, which may seem obscure to some, is easily traced; for the songs which accompany the games generally have reference to facts of the animal or vegetable life familiar to the children, and which are a part also of that later knowledge. They tell sometimes of the seed-time or the harvest, sometimes of the dogs or cows, the sheep, or the fowls and pigeons that come to be fed. The child's interest is thus excited in his immediate surroundings. He quickly wants to know more about them, and to noting the difference between field and garden, wood and common, hill and flat ground, pond and running water, is but a step. The transition-class takes up this same familiar knowledge, and carries it on to the first notion of local topography, and thence to the first outline of physical geography, which, later, will make historical geography intelligible and useful, instead of being a mere list of names. The child has been led on, step by step, to acquire the knowledge he had come to wish for, and each step has helped to make a track he will only need to continue.

It is time now to turn our attention to the other two fundamental forms—the cube and the cylinder—which we have here on the right and left of the table. All the so-called *occupations* of the kindergarten, all that series of work by which the children are trained to accuracy of sight and manipulation while acquiring familiarity with the elements of arithmetic, with geometrical forms, and the beauty of symmetrical design, begin here, as the children learn to distinguish the various lines and angles, the surfaces and peculiarities generally of these two fundamental forms, to reproduce them, and develop other figures from them. Madame de Portugall, as we see, divides the occupations derived respectively from the cube and the cylinder into four groups, according as their starting point is either the solid itself, the surface, the line, or the point. All four groups are found under the head of the cube, three only, solids, lines, and surfaces, under that of the cylinder. *Points* are first distinguished by the child in the sharp corner of the cube, and therefore such occupations as deal with separate points or dots, as, for instance, bead-work, pricking, etc., belong to the cube-series only.

Let us begin with the solids. There we find modelling again in both series; the difference as it is practised in the one or the other being in the different forms, *whether circular or rectangular*, that are copied in each. Building, on the other hand, which is exclusively carried on with rectangular pieces, belongs to the cube-series only. If we follow up the lines from both these sections to the school work, we find that what has been learned in this manner from the cube and the cylinder, leads up to geometry. The table indicates this, as usual, by the colour of the lines—the vertical lines being of the same blue that marks geometry in the school division. When we come to surfaces, some of the most important occupations, such as paper cutting, paper folding, are common to both series; they only take different directions according as they deal wholly with surfaces bounded by straight lines, as when derived from the cube, or by partly straight and partly curved lines, as when derived from the cylinder. In the first series they lead up again, as we see, to geometry, in the second to drawing and needlework. Paper plaiting, one of the favourite occupations of the younger children, opens a field for instruction in various branches; it leads up to arithmetic from the skill it gives in counting, to drawing from the initiation to symmetrical design, to needlework from the manual dexterity it requires. This belongs to the cube-series, only dealing exclusively with rectangular figures. Occupations based on the study of lines only, differ very much one from the other in the two series. The cube gives us a great variety, of which some, the stick-laying, the laths, and the linear drawing, form a most important part of kindergarten instruction, and which earliest develop the child's intelligence, as they lead him to compare the direction of lines, the shape and magnitude of figures, and to become familiar with geometrical lines and angles, and forms, and with their correct names. Some will think the latter acquisition is of but little use to him now, but they forget that thus we open one more ingress to the inevitably harder studies of later years. For when those children come to a school lesson of geometry, one great difficulty will have been surmounted. The terms used will have a meaning to them; to them these figures will be real things, which they have handled and constructed, and they will be all the further on the way to learning their properties and uses. In the cylinder-series, under the group *lines*, we find thread-laying and metal rings; curved surfaces being produced by the former, in preparation for learning to trace them with a pencil; and the rings and sections of rings introduce altogether a new element, both into the designing of patterns, and into the study of lines and forms. For here we have the circle and its divisions, with the angles formed at the centre, and the names for all these new things to be acquired, and endless new designs to be invented.

This table enables us to see at a glance what immense variety of occupations have been planned in the kindergarten based upon the elements provided for us by these two fundamental forms; and those to whom the whole subject is new will, I believe, with the aid of some good diagrams of the occupations mentioned, learn more of the *motives* of the system by viewing its parts thus grouped and arranged, than by going at once to see the practical work. They would, of course, understand any one occupation better by seeing it worked at a kindergarten, but they will get a better idea of the whole of the educational value of the entire method by first studying this table. On the other hand, those who are familiar with the practical working, and can at once fill up the detail, will often acquire a new insight into the principles by having thus brought before them the connection, link by link, of earlier and later instruction, and seeing side by side in each group the natural position of these occupations, which to many appear isolated; which many teachers even treat as mere exercises, more or less ingenious, that might be taken up in any order, and chosen from at random. This table demonstrates their order, a necessary one, springing from a fundamental idea, and it also shows their relative importance, enabling us, when we have mastered the principle, to distinguish rapidly groups devoted to the same purpose, that which affords the most fruitful development of the principle, or which points to the most important results. If this were a lecture on the merits of the kindergarten system generally, it would be needful to enter more closely into the value of each occupation as it influences the whole; but my object this evening is simply to bring prominently forward the unity of the system, not merely within itself, but as part of an all-embracing system of human culture, and to draw attention, as I have said, to the use of this table in making this fact manifest. I will not, however, leave the subject of the occupations without pointing out to those who are only superficially acquainted with the kindergarten what minute pains Fröbel took to devise the means of drawing out in children their faculties of observation, judgment, and activity. Now he is not content to do this through one kind of work, but through many kinds; not in one direction, but in many directions. Each of these occupations has its own special object, but it has also that common object in view—each one helps to lay a foundation for acquiring knowledge, now of number, now of form, now of natural history; and it combines with all the other occupations and amusements, in developing the latent power of the infant intellect and will. And once more, I think that as we thus look at the detail of the kindergarten training as it is given us here arranged in its natural groups, we form a better idea of the goal to which every portion of that detail tends; a goal beyond the school to which we see the instruction immediately pointing, beyond the higher instruction to which the school studies stretch out, to that real goal of all human life and endeavour—the perfecting of the whole nature for the active service of God and man.

If we return now to the synoptical table, leaving the kindergarten, we come to the space contained between two horizontal lines which designates the school period of study. Children of the classes above those who attend the elementary infant schools generally go to school at seven or eight years old. They have, perhaps, already some acquaintance with the art of reading; a certain number of these, whose parents have been most careful, will know even something of writing and counting; all the rest the schoolmaster has to teach. Nor does it matter how little they know—his whole success depends not on their power of reading words of two syllables, but on their *power of learning;* and whether he has to teach arithmetic or grammar, geometry or geography—he must draw largely on the faculty of observation, of comparison and judgment—and he finds them all unused to exercise. He wants accuracy of hand and eye for writing, and drawing, and needlework; pliancy of limb and attention to time for gymnastic exercises; and he has to work with stiff and feeble fingers, with ears unused to time, and eyes unused to form. But, on the other hand, if his pupils come to him at eight years old from the kindergarten, with its transition classes, then, as this table shows us, each branch of necessary instruction rests upon a foundation already acquired, or is aided by faculties already exercised.

We all know what the general programme of school instruction is, and we have it in outline here. It may be gathered under three groups:—*Language*, represented at first by the mother-tongue, and grammar, and general history; the science of form and number, represented by arithmetic, geometry, and drawing; and natural science, beginning with natural history and cosmography. To these may, indeed should be, added music and gymnastics for both sexes, and needlework for girls. These are valuable as portions of the training of the active powers and of the senses which school education so sadly neglects. The most indispensable instruction must embrace the three groups enumerated above, and all further instruction takes its departure from them. Now, if we look at the table and notice the colour of the lines which are traced under each school subject, we see the lines similarly coloured coming up from below from some branch of kindergarten training, higher amid the games or occupations which were derived from one or other of the three fundamental forms; and this kindergarten work has trained the very aptitude required for such or such branch of school work, or laid down the first lines of the knowledge school instruction purports to impart. Nothing, as you see, which is brought before the schoolboy (or girl) is absolutely strange to him. It is, indeed, leading him to the unknown, but it is linked to the known. As compared with the labour of the untrained children, it is like learning a new piece of poetry in one's own tongue as compared with learning a series of words in a foreign language. Once more let me point out how this table helps to fix attention on that most important fact, of the connexion of all the apparently trivial occupations of a nursery class with the difficult lessons and discipline of school years, and through them with the wider studies and experience which finally fit man out for the highest moral and intellectual labour. Opponents of the system, or careless observers, may, perhaps, say that continuity is in one sense a natural and inevitable one; whatever a child learns by himself, or from others, the story he reads, the sum he is forced to do, the animals that he sees around him, the weary grammar over which he sheds his tears, are all connected, somehow or other, with the knowledge of later years, is absorbed into it, and becomes a part of the intellectual store. Yes—*somehow or other!* But with Fröbel it is purposed beforehand—it is done in orderly sequence; and each game or occupation has its special object of exercising some faculty, of cultivating some quality, in a methodical manner for future use, and to do this through the means of instruction which lays the methodical foundation for future instruction.

And if a table like this could mark the moral growth, as it marks the lines of intellectual development, we should see that the qualities most needed by boy and man—the patient resolution that overcomes difficulties, the love of truth—that is cultivated by perfect accuracy of work and expression, the kindly feelings generated by sharing the work and success of others, freedom of thought and invention which lead to respecting the work and the freedom of others, reverence for all greatness and goodness which is the germ of religion—are casting their roots into the character by the aid of that same early discipline, ready to expand and strengthen as life becomes freer and richer in action and opportunities.

We have nearly completed our survey of the table. We have examined it through the portion devoted to the kindergarten, through the school portion, and, finally, we may trace the upper branches of this tree of culture, whose root is in the ball games. Those branches are still gathered in the same groups, only modified as they enlarge. Language now embraces literature and all that bears on human life and conduct tending to the highest philosophy; science becomes wider in some directions, and more abstract in others; the study of form becomes the study of the fine arts; and in this highest stage of their progress, while each branch demands more special cultivation, yet the links that bind them all become more apparent. The close affinities that underlie all sections of the great field of knowledge begin to be felt, and amid the widest divergencies of special researches there is seen to be a higher harmony in which they converge in the same great search for truth. Lord Bacon has somewhere made a fine remark on the different order of minds that love to seek resemblances or differences, the latter occupying the larger number; while the higher toned minds seek the resemblance in which apparent differences meet and rise above men's knowledge to philosophy and the higher efforts of imagination. It is the same with the course of human culture as men advance towards the full development of their nature. While special studies demand their time and claim the exercise of special aptitudes, the mind accustomed to the exercise of all its powers cannot be thus limited in its interests and sympathies, and tends more and more, as the nature ripens and expands, to rise from the lower ground of separate action, to the higher level of philosophic thought and union.

To few is it given to reach these serene heights; but indefinitely higher than it now is might be the stand-point of all, if education were systematically directed to the full development of each man's nature, according to the means of his natural faculties and opportunities; if no conventional barriers, no dreary morass of neglect, hemmed in the mental growth. How many, now blind to any necessary connection between morals and knowledge, between active life and a life of contemplation or study, how many wandering in apparently opposing tracks of work and opinion, would, if so educated, be able at least to feel the unity of all separate endeavours to read the laws of God as inscribed on the face of nature and in the heart of man, and recognize the duty of living in willing obedience to them.

To keep this foremost as the ideal of life is the true purpose of education, to which all special cultivation, all men's acquirements, must ever be subordinate. Fröbel never loses sight of this purpose, and from the cradle, from the ball games with the infants, to the fulness of self-conscious endeavours in the highest pursuits of science and philosophy, directs us ceaselessly to it. If then Madame de Portugall by this visible outline of his system helps to make this, his highest aim, more clearly manifest, to keep it more distinctly before the minds of all kindergarten teachers, we may gladly accept her help, and thank her for this new service to the cause.

THE USE OF STORIES

IN THE

KINDERGARTEN.

By ANNA BUCKLAND.

AMONGST the great thinkers who have planned schemes of education, Fröbel, above all others, founds his system on the wide principle, that the highest type of humanity which education can produce is reached by the equal and simultaneous growth of every faculty. He studies the child as it is, taking it as from God, and on the knowledge gained by close and patient observation of the child's nature, he plans a system of development the result of which is to be, not the expression of an individual educator's ideal of humanity, but the full, rich, harmonious life of every faculty, the germs of which he finds in the child. Hence Fröbel's system provides for the nourishment of every root in its earliest stage, on the ground, that all are essential to a noble, perfect growth, and that one-sided culture at any stage produces contraction and deformity.

Starting from these two fundamental principles—first, that the development of every faculty existing in the child is essential for the production of the highest type of humanity; and, secondly, that for perfect, harmonious development there must be simultaneous growth—we are not surprised to find that in Fröbel's system æsthetic culture occupies at starting a large space.

He notices that, of all the mental faculties, the æsthetic is one of the first to unfold in the mind of a child; and he concludes, therefore, that its training and culture have immediate claims on the educator. Whatever the use of æsthetics may be to the child in the work of gaining the means of material existence in future life, is not in question; the fact that the faculty is there, is sufficient to show that it is one of the essential roots by means of which the child's nature receives nourishment, needful for its perfect, healthy, vigorous growth. Fröbel does not presume, therefore, to treat æsthetics as the mere ornaments of life—" the efflorescence of civilization," as Herbert Spencer calls them—the culture of which may be deferred to some far distant day of idle leisure in a future, golden age, in order meantime to press forward the studies necessary for the preservation and maintenance of material existence. "When," says Herbert Spencer, "the forces of Nature have been fully conquered to man's use, when the means of production have been brought to perfection, when labour has been economized to the highest degree, when education has been so systematized that a preparation for the more essential activities may be made with comparative rapidity, and when consequently there is a great increase of spare time, then will the Beautiful both in Art and Nature rightly fill a large space in the minds of all."

If it were possible to contract education into a training, which had for its first object the obtaining of the means for improved material existence, we might ask whether the race so trained were likely to have any large space of mind left, to be filled by Beauty, in the idle years, after Nature had been forced to contribute all she could to man's material prosperity. A civilization which was separated from æsthetics would tend rather to "lay waste our powers," and lead us on at last to say—

> " Little we see in Nature that is ours,
> We have given our hearts away, a sordid boon,
> This sea, that bares her bosom to the moon,
> The winds, that will be howling at all hours,
> And are up-gathered now like sleeping flowers,
> For this—for everything, we are out of tune ;
> It moves us not." . . . .

But a one-sided system of education, even when advanced by so earnest and noble a thinker as Herbert Spencer, must in the end be counteracted by Nature herself, who, by continually re-asserting her power, defeats all attempts to cramp her energies in any direction. The vitality of the æsthetic faculty cannot be extinguished by any system which denies it culture, much as it may lose in truth of action for lack of due training. Early history and early literature prove to us that the sense of the Beautiful in Nature and in character wakes into vigorous life before man begins to concern himself about the material wealth laid up in Nature's storehouse, or to seek to turn it to his use through intellect and labour. It is the same in individual life ; the first perceptions of the child are of beauty. The baby crows with delight at the beauty of the round, silvery moon in the dark sky, and the little child gazes with tender love at the beauty of the daisies in the green grass, long before he concerns himself as to the relation to his physical life of the heavenly bodies and of the productions of the earth.

Those who believe with Fröbel that each little child is a thought of God will readily grant that this early unfolding of the æsthetic faculty is a part of the Divine plan ; for it is by means of this faculty that, as soon as the knowledge of God is presented to the little child, he is able to perceive at once the beauty of goodness in the Divine character, and the sense of this beauty calls forth emotions of admiration, love, joy, and reverence.

We see, therefore, why Fröbel gives so large a space in his system to æsthetic culture; and why he places it at once under the hands of the skilled educator. He sees how this faculty is one of the essential roots on which growth depends, that it must be supplied at once with fitting nourishment; and he perceives that it is connected with the most solemn relations and duties of human existence. We find, therefore, in the Kindergarten, that the means are provided by which the æsthetic faculty may be developed and trained to a keen perception of beauty in form, colour, and sound, as well as in character and life. Artistic design, lessons on form, combinations of colours, drawing, modelling in clay, flowers and beautiful natural objects, music, poetry, and imaginative literature, are all provided, as necessary to the earliest education of the child. It is of the imaginative literature alone that we now have to speak.

A glance at Madame de Portugall's synoptical table shows us that the line which in later education is marked as literature is reached from stories in the Kindergarten. Literature is thus recognized as necessary at starting for the complete development of the child. It is not to be regarded merely as a source of amusement, but is to be placed among the essentials of education. We may notice here the deeper insight which Fröbel has into the nature of children, as well as into the meaning and purposes of literature, if we observe the view which Professor Bain takes of imaginative literature in his scheme of education. He sees in it only "a means for indulging the emotions"—"an ingredient in the satisfaction of life," and goes on—"In addition to our enjoyment gained from realities, we crave for the contribution to our enjoyment which comes from ideality. Now Ideality is a different thing for different ages, fairy tales and extravaganzas for the young; the Poetry of Milton for the old. There is nothing educative in the first instance, we are not aiming at instruction, but drinking in emotion. The gratifying of children with the Literature of Imagination is a matter for the parent, as much as giving them country walks, or holiday treats."

It is true that the education of a child is by no means confined to the school-room; and the purposes which imaginative literature serves may be answered by the stories given to children by thoughtful parents, as well as by their use in the Kindergarten. The point of difference between Fröbel and Bain is not, whether stories are to be given in or out of the school-room, but whether they are to be called "educative." And the reason why Professor Bain denies this term to imaginative literature is, that he does not hold the æsthetic faculty to be one of those roots, the constant and fitting nourishment of which is essential to the perfect growth and development of the whole being. He regards the æsthetic faculty as one that may very well be left out of education altogether, which serves no great purpose in life, and is only a means for an increase of selfish enjoyment. It is against this view that we give some of the uses of stories in the Kindergarten; admitting that the same ends may be served by stories at home; but especially urging that they should be used as means of development and training, and not as a mere holiday gratification: for if the stories of childhood are to be sought as a means only for exciting emotion, and put out of the sphere of education altogether, the line of stories will not lead up to Milton in older life, but to the sensational novel, or gossiping journal.

In giving some of the chief uses of stories in the Kindergarten, we are at the same time using arguments for the study of literature in later education; but it must not be forgotten that there are many important advantages in the study of our best writers, besides those gained in the early use of stories.

Stories are the child's first introduction into that grand world of the ideal in character and life; and the first and highest use of stories is to enable a child to form a pure and noble ideal of what man may be and do. A child who is taught only certain moral precepts, and who has no representation put before him of these truths expressed in characters and actions, rising above the common level, will lack the courage, the energy, the aspiration, and still more the humility, necessary to raise his own character and life to the highest standard—

> "We live by Admiration, Hope, and Love,
> And even as these are well and wisely fixed,
> In dignity of being we ascend."

A second use of stories is in the illustrations they supply to children of the laws governing life. The lessons of experience are only learnt in the course of years; and children have at once to begin to live in a world in which they are strangers. We may tell children that certain causes produce certain effects, but the lesson is soon forgotten; if the law, however, is shown in action in a story, the consequences remain fixed in the mind, and again and again through life serve as a guide under similar circumstances. An intelligent old gardener, whose family are now risen in the world and well known, used to read to his children directions for conduct from the Bible, and then illustrate these by stories from Shakespeare's Plays: and this showing of the great truths of life in their proper action in the world gave the lessons a living power, that could not pass away.

A third use of stories is the sense they give a child of a world beyond his own; and thus, next to companionship, they serve to destroy that egotism which looks on self as centre of all things. The child perceives that he stands in brotherly relation to children he has never seen or known, but who enjoy what he does, who have the same difficulties and temptations to overcome, and from this knowledge spring up a genial love for others and the cheerful courage that the sense of companionship gives.

A fourth use of stories is for the development of sympathy, or the imagination of the heart. Stories bring before a child a large amount of human experience, with which he would otherwise be unfamiliar; but by the help of imagination he can conceive what others suffer or enjoy; and thus, without unduly exciting emotion, it can be kept in healthy exercise; and the child is trained to quickness of perception in regard to the feelings of others, and is prepared for entering into joys and sorrows beyond his actual range of experience.

A fifth use of stories is in bringing the power of example to bear upon children. The true influence of example, we must notice, is not that of a pattern to be copied; children should not be encouraged to practise direct imitations of particular actions, which are held up to admiration, because this leads only to a petty vain attempt to repeat what has been admired, in hope of getting the same applause. But the real power of example lies in the special inspiration it gives to a particular principle of conduct. For this reason, the best example stories are those taken from times or countries in which life was different from the present, so that the action may not be literally repeated, but that it may rather rouse to greater vigour the principle or feeling upon which the special action was founded. The story of the good Samaritan, with its close, "Go and do likewise," illustrates the true meaning and force of example stories.

In the use of stories in the Kindergarten, it is important that the stock should not be too large. The repetition of a story is not tedious to children. They delight in an old story, for all the world is new to them, and they seek a rest from novelty in familiarity; just as, when the world grows old to us, we seek a change from monotony in novelty. An old story has a growing influence upon children, whilst the first effect of a new story is often scarcely felt. In fact a good story cannot be thoroughly understood, nor can it answer all the purposes it is meant to serve, until it has been repeated many times. The notion that children's stories have in them nothing educative, that they are to be classed only among the gratifications of life, has led to their being supplied to children in such abundance that they are often only skipped through and thrown aside. One strong plea for the use of stories in the Kindergarten is, that they may be really studied and understood, so as to serve for the true development and training of the child, and not for the undue stimulation of the imagination into a spurious, irregular life. It is scarcely necessary to say that the stories selected for the Kindergarten should be true to the principles of good literature; that they should be simple and free from casuistry, false sentiment, and exaggerations of every kind; that they should be of bright and delicate fancy, sweet, tender, and true.

A short analysis of children's literature may, perhaps, be helpful in guiding the choice of stories for the Kindergarten. We will divide it into the usual classes of Ideal, or purely imaginative literature, and Realistic, or having a form taken from life in the actual world. Under the head of imaginative literature, we place fairy-stories, allegories, and fables. We will take the composition of a fairy-story first, not only because a fairy-story has the greatest charm for children, but also because it is really one of the higher forms of literature. The idea in the minds of many story-tellers, and story-writers too, is that a fairy-story means any jumble of incidents, in which for no distinct purpose or design natural laws are set at defiance. But the very meaning of the word "faerie" is spiritual; and if we analyze one of the genuine old fairy-stories, we shall nearly always find that there is at the heart of it some great spiritual truth, which forms the soul, as it were, of the story. The incidents of the story are all designed for the purpose of showing this truth in action; and what makes it " faerie " is, that in order to give the freest scope for the working out of the truth, fancy may create a world for the action of it—a world in which there is no restriction from natural laws and material necessities. It is in fact a kind of superior action given to spirit over matter.

We may illustrate the composition of a true fairy-story by a brief analysis of " The Sleeping Beauty." The inner truth at the heart of this story is, that hatred works death—" he that hateth his brother is a murderer "—but love is stronger than hatred, and it is through love alone that the works of hatred are to be destroyed. First there is the christening of the new child; at the very beginning its life is threatened by the hatred of the malignant fairy, out of revenge because she was not invited to the feast. The child is to die, though the curse is afterwards changed into the death-like sleep, which is death as regards all the purposes of life. The king tries to defeat the curse of hatred by the unspiritual means of destroying all the spindles in his kingdom; but this, of course, is of no avail. The day comes when, in spite of this precaution, the maiden finds the wicked fairy spinning. She takes the spindle, pricks herself, and immediately sinks with all the world around her into the death-like sleep. Around the castle grows the thick hedge of thorns and briers, as high as the towers, so that it cannot be leapt over; and this is set by hatred to prevent the entrance of love into the world of death. Then one after another the princes come; they wish to see the beauty of the sleeping maiden; but this desire cannot carry them through the thorns and briers. A hundred years pass away, and the curse of hatred still works; time, that all things else destroys, has in itself no power to impair the strength of the curse. At last, in due time, the true prince appears. He is counselled by prudent people not to try to enter the castle, for he cannot do so but through suffering, and the end may be only death. But the prospect of suffering, or death, cannot daunt him; love is stronger than fear and the instinct of self-preservation. He approaches the hedge, and the thorns and briers are to him but as fragrant roses—this is the first victory of love over the obstacles placed by hatred in the way of its ultimate triumph. The roses close behind him, and become again thorns and briers; love can carry him forward, but there is no smoothing of the way for retreat. At length he enters the castle. The whole world within shares in the sleep of death. The dogs in the castle-yard, the pigeons on the roof, the flies on the window-panes, the servants in the kitchen, the courtiers, the king and the queen, all lie under the power of hatred. At the first expression of a love which can "give and hazard all," the whole world of death wakes to life, with the freshness and vigour of a new spring-day. The deadly curse of hatred is destroyed; thought and work are filled with energy; everything is in action. "And they all lived happily to the end," is the conclusion of the fine old story.

If we analyze in the same way any other of the genuine old fairy-stories, such as "Cinderella," or "Mrs. Holle," we shall find that the play of fancy is not the mere irregular wandering of a dream, but that there is distinct unity of design in the incidents, while at the heart of all of them lies some great immortal truth, which gives them their hold on generation after generation, and will preserve them in the perpetual freshness of child-like beauty as long as the world shall last.

It is in contrasting the old fairy-stories with such books as "Alice's Adventures in Wonderland" that we feel the more strongly the artistic perfection of the old stories. Natural laws and ordinary combinations are set aside in the Alice books, not that fancy may have free scope to create a world for the working out of any great spiritual truth, but only for the sake of the odd effect which incongruity produces. It is Wonderland, but it is not Fairyland. There is humour in the incongruity; but it requires familiarity with ordinary laws and combinations to feel the humour of incongruity; and children are much less struck with the odd effect than older people; as a little child once asked—" Why *shouldn't* a walrus go out with a carpenter?" Children miss also the slight satire which underlies some parts, and, together with the humour, gives to the bright fancy of these books a charm for older readers.

Allegories are more spiritualized than fairy-stories, and have less of human interest. In an allegory, the personages of the story are not human beings, but represent single abstract qualities. The scene also of the story, though taken from the material world, is composed of objects, most of which are symbols. There is consequently less unity of idea, and less unity of art, in the construction of an allegory. They serve good purpose in direct religious teaching, and in moral training. They are useful also in training children to understand symbols, and to see readily the relation of form to essence, and the fitness of certain material things to express abstract qualities. This will prepare them, not only for the later study of our great classic allegories of English literature, but also for the understanding of poetry, and of many parts of the Bible ; and will enable them to see in Nature, not only the beauty of material form, but the deep truths she teaches, so that—" The earth and common face of Nature." may speak to them " rememberable things."

Fables are stories of imagination, in that speech is given to animals. The essence of a fable is the representation of the faults and follies of human beings, as reflected in the sayings and doings of the lower creation. A fable is therefore necessarily a satire; and this is an element of literature which it would be dangerous for children to learn to love for its own sake. It requires, therefore, careful use in the Kindergarten, and should be reserved only for minor faults common among the children themselves. A good-natured, hearty laugh at the reflection of ourselves in a fable is a very wholesome thing; but if the laugh is a sneer at humanity, there is a fear of destroying reverence and love.

Realistic stories are those best fitted for illustrating the laws by which life is governed, and thus showing to children that the consequences which follow conduct are as sure as the sequence of cause and effect. A good realistic story should consist of one general law of life, shown in its ordinary legitimate action. The scenes for the action must be the real world of human character and life. Though a realistic story is thus a sketch from nature, it must be a *picture*, and not a mere *photograph*. The attempt to imitate exactly the sayings and doings of children, as in the books called "Helen's Babies" and "Totty's Book," though very amusing to read, is not real literature, because there is no artistic purpose or design in them. Jane Austen's novels are some of the best examples in literature of good realistic stories. There is in each a distinct, intelligent purpose, which is artistically worked out in characters and scenes, drawn entirely from the living around her.

As one object of realistic stories for children is to accustom them to expect certain results as the consequences of certain actions, it is important that they should deal with the simple, ordinary laws of life, and not with paradoxes or exceptions. In mature literature it has been the work of some of the finest master-hands to show how the action of a lower law may be on occasions set aside by the intervention of a higher, and that we have to take into consideration a wider range in predicting results; but exceptions only puzzle children, who use them at once for generalizing, and it is important to establish first the general law as the common rule for conduct. Extraordinary stories, in which wholly inadequate means are represented as producing desired results, lay the foundations of idleness and recklessness of consequences in after life, and are the cause of much bad work and senseless disregard of natural laws. Perfect truthfulness to nature is essential in a good realistic story. The incidents must be such as naturally follow certain causes; the characters must represent real, living children of the true type, not precocious exceptions; and the feeling must be neither of a kind unusual in a child, nor of a degree beyond what the situation requires. Children so soon detect falseness, and every attempt to produce impression by exaggeration wakens distrust in the mind of a child, almost unconsciously to himself.

A realistic story for children must not only be true to life, but the characters and scenes should be taken from that portion of life which belongs to children. It is a principle of the best school of literature, that all subjects are not subjects for art; because art has a purpose of its own, which is not answered by the merely artistic treatment of every kind of subject. The highest function of art is to lead the mind to the love of the beautiful in nature and human life; and in mature literature the glory of the highest ideal cannot be shown without showing the hard conflict, the upward struggle through darkness and evil to the last victory of light and duty; but the introduction of mature evil into children's literature, before they have to enter into conflict with it, and before faith has taken such root as to assure the final victory of good, has a most injurious and depressing effect upon a child's mind. It is needful for the Kindergarten teacher to keep this in mind, because so many stories for children have appeared of late depicting the low current of London life, and dealing, not with the faults of childhood, but with the mature sins of drunkenness, brutality, and coarse vice. True temperance stories for children are those in which the nobleness of self-denial and control over appetite is shown; and feelings of compassion for the erring are most truly and effectually trained in childhood by calling out pity for a companion in age who has yielded to a mutual temptation. The world of the poor belongs to the life of children; and stories of the poor, of the hardships they have to endure, are useful in awakening sympathy; there are also in such stories to be found the highest examples of patience and unselfish love.

Stories that belong to other subjects of culture have also their place in the Kindergarten; but these may be left to their own special lines. Such are Bible stories, natural history stories, stories of travel and adventure, biography or history.

It has been taken for granted that, in using stories in the Kindergarten, the stories are read by the teacher, and told to the children. It is sometimes said that telling stories is a gift; but it is only an art, more easy at first to some persons than to others. The chief reason why some persons cannot tell stories is because they have "no story to tell." They have only a dim, confused picture of one in the mind, and the first thing to be done is to get this vague image perfectly clear and vivid. For this purpose, it will be necessary for them to read the story over several times; and in order to be sure that the impression is strong enough to reproduce it accurately, and *without any hesitation*, it may be useful to write it from memory, and compare it with the original.

The next thing is to look for the leading idea, or inner truth, of the story, and then mark the strong points of the narrative. They are the features that express the soul, as it were, and in telling the story they will require the greatest prominence; and if the teacher supplies additional details, these should all tend to the further illustration of the leading idea. Children love details, but unnecessary particulars only confuse, and destroy effect. If, for instance, a room has to be described, the first point to be determined is what idea the room has to express, as poverty, cheerfulness, disorder; and then only such details as strengthen the idea, and conform to it, need be given. Teachers who picture Bible scenes often quite destroy the effect of the narrative, because they do not preserve the relation between the details they supply and the leading idea of the story.

It is better in narration to keep to one single line, and avoid episodes; for children easily lose a thread; and if their interest has once been diverted, it is difficult for them to return to the former line. It is often necessary, therefore, to sacrifice the idea of the simultaneous action of two lines of narration in order to complete one, before taking up the other. For instance, in telling the story of the First Book of Spenser's "Faerie Queene," to a class of children from twelve to fourteen, it was found necessary, at the part where the Red Cross Knight and Una are separated, to continue the adventures of the Red Cross Knight up to the point where he meets Una again, and then to take up Una's story, and tell that continuously to the same point. Spenser, it will be remembered, preserves the idea of simultaneous action, by taking up the story of each in alternate cantos; but children, even of that age, were incapable of carrying on the two lines of narrative at the same time, and tangled the threads of the story. It is desirable in the repetition of a story to keep as nearly as possible to the first version of it. Children see at once the details of a story, and retain a vivid impression of them in the inward eye. They are always ready to correct the slightest deviation from the original with a serious air of reproof, for it is associated in their minds with a want of truthfulness. Thus in telling a story, it was once said, there were *three* plates on the shelf. Every bright little mental eye saw the three plates, as plainly as possible; and when, on repeating the story, it was said there were *two* plates on the shelf, an indignant exclamation at once arose,—"There were *three* plates, last time there were *three* plates." A charitable little child suggested, "But perhaps one has been broken since last time"; the general feeling, however, was, that the second version was not strictly truthful.

Conversations have much more effect if related in the first person; and this form also gives the story-teller opportunity for varying the voice and manner, according to the character of the speaker. Children always begin to brighten into eager interest directly the story becomes dramatic; and more feeling can be given to the touching passages.

The use of expectation and surprise is helpful in keeping up the interest of little children, and questions and guesses recall their attention at once, if it should have wandered. If, however, these are used too much, children sometimes become rather confused between the guesses of the class and the facts of the story.

The difficulty of telling stories to children is one which, like all others, disappears by practice. Persons who are unaccustomed to be with children often fancy they cannot tell stories, but if they only get the outlines of one story thoroughly and clearly impressed in their own minds, and repeat this story a few times to children, they will find that very soon they can tell it easily and well. They can then in the same way try another and another. It has been well said that the best way, when you think you cannot do a thing, is to go and do it. And certainly there is no art in the world which can be learned only from directions, nor is there any talent so great that it can attain success without practice. In the majority of cases, it is impossible for any one to decide that he is lacking in the necessary ability for any art until he has done his best for some time to acquire it. If a Kindergarten teacher believes she has no gift for telling stories, let her try what she can do without a gift, and the probability is, that she will find herself more richly endowed than she thought she was. It used to be said that teaching was a gift, and so in a certain sense it is; but we are beginning to find out that it is a gift which nearly every good and loving woman possesses, only she may not at once know just how to use it. The very love for little children, and the sympathy with them, which lie at the heart of the Kindergarten system, will teach its teachers how to put before the minds of children bright pictures from that grand world of the ideal in which the little ones often seem to be more at home than in the real.

In taking up in this paper the single line of imaginative literature in the Kindergarten scheme, it will readily be understood that no plea is put forward for giving it any other than its due place amongst those subjects which help to promote harmonious growth and development. No comparison is intended between the claims of literature and science as agents of education; because both are believed to be of equal necessity to the formation of a complete character, and to a preparation for the duty and work of life. In a system of education which has a place for every God-given faculty of man, there can be no attempt at estimating education values, so as to bring one class of subjects forward to the neglect of another. The Kindergarten system says rather, with Milton, "Let us be humbly wise." Let us take the little child as a thought of God, and in faith and trust cultivate every faculty of its nature; assured that the realization of the Divine ideal in humanity must be its highest type, and that the man or woman, who is most capable of a full, rich, complete life as an individual, is most fitted for advancing the progress of the race in all the best work of this world, as well as best prepared for all that may be beyond this world of immortal growth and work.

ON THE

PHYSICAL EDUCATION OF GIRLS.

By FRANCES E. HOGGAN, M.D.

I HAVE chosen the physical education of girls for consideration to-night, because it is a subject most fit to engage the attention of all friends of the Kindergarten, from the fact that the need for such education for girls begins when they pass out of the Kindergarten or the nursery into the schoolroom. While in the Kindergarten they have very properly their instruction, their exercise, and their play, in common with little boys; and it would, I believe, be well if this life in common were continued, under careful supervision, through later childhood. We have, however, to take things as we find them, and to consider the special needs of girls in respect of physical education in the present state of society in England, where co-education of the sexes is discountenanced by the majority of unthinking and by some thinking persons, and where, in general, the proper adjustments are wanting which would make co-education of the sexes both harmless and profitable.

Infants need only be allowed to kick and fling about their little limbs freely, untrammelled by tight or voluminous clothing. Their life is spent between sleep, food, and exercise, with a large margin for the latter. Sickly infants ever require medical supervision chiefly in order that their sur roundings may be wisely regulated, suitable food, air, and exercise ensured, and the infant organism placed in the best possible conditions for returning to the healthy standard from which some mischance has caused it to deviate. Healthy infants do not require systematized gymnastic exercises. If their limbs are allowed full play, they will invent the best of exercises for themselves, some of them complicated and comical enough, as, for instance, the feat common to all babies, and which no physical educator has ever attempted to rival, of thrusting the toes into the mouth—a feat which requires for its successful accomplishment much steady and persevering preparatory exercise of whole groups of muscles. Sickly infants may require parts of their muscular system to be specially acted upon and strengthened, so as to restore the lost balance and bring all parts of the body into harmonious relation, but healthy infants will thrive all the better for a little of that wholesome neglect which consists in letting them play and even use their left hand unchecked. It has been well said by a wise friend of children :* "We may leave the infant to nature for exercise ; it will be well attended to and carried through an efficient course of training, reaching every muscle of the body, which we should find it difficult to imitate by art."

Little children in a Kindergarten intelligently conducted may be said to live in an atmosphere of healthful activity. Daily orderly exercise gives them such command over their various groups of muscles that they accomplish with unconscious vigour and grace movements which the untrained child goes through clumsily and awkwardly, the clumsiness and awkwardness resulting from a want of co-ordination in the contraction of muscles which must act together with great delicacy, in obedience to a common impulse communicated from the will, in order to execute many apparently simple movements, such as shaking hands, drawing on a slate, marching, halting

* Dr. Elizabeth Blackwell, "Lectures on the Laws of Life," 1871.

suddenly, &c. Of course, little children who grow up in the country, and lead a free out-door life, sliding, jumping, swimming, climbing trees, throwing stones, and engaging in all kinds of work and of laborious play, may acquire such control over their muscular system as leaves little to be desired. It is the great merit of the Kindergarten that it is adapted to the wants of town-bred children, debarred from such natural pastimes, as well as to the wants of indolent, ungainly children, and that it renders even the latter apt to execute without awkwardness a great variety of combined movements either slowly, quickly, or with moderate quickness; apt, in short, to exercise control over their whole muscular apparatus, and to adjust it to the requirements of their will.

The senses, too, which in the majority of little town-bred children of the middle and upper classes are cut off from an adequate supply of objects on which to exercise themselves, and by exercise to develop steadily and healthfully, are methodically trained in the Kindergarten into habits of activity, strengthened by daily pleasurable use, and sharpened by carefully planned exercises and games, which, while they educate, afford at the same time much innocent amusement and delight.

While on the subject of Kindergartens it may not be out of place to insist on one indispensable condition of their success, viz. that they be intelligently conducted by able, cultured, and efficiently trained women. To give the necessary professional training is the aim of the recently founded London Kindergarten Training College; and it is the earnest hope of its founders that it may be the means of educating a band of faithful, devoted, large-minded, and large-hearted Kindergarten teachers, who will go out into the English-speaking world as missionaries of the educational reform which Fröbel inaugurated, and which appeals so powerfully to the best instincts and sympathies of every mother's heart. This reform must be worked for, I again repeat, intelligently and reasonably by adapting the Kindergarten system to the special circumstances of every country, by modifying details of management when found necessary, by allowing even of the possibility of further development in the future. In short, Fröbel must take his proper place as a great reformer, an enthusiastic and enlightened friend of little children, who systematized and simplified the educational methods which the best mothers and teachers of all ages, led by their intuitive perception of the requirements of very young children, have always been in the habit of employing. He must *not* be set up as an idol to be blindly worshipped and implicitly obeyed, whose precepts are to supersede reason and common sense, and to silence their questionings. This would be to erect a fetish, not to choose a guide, and the Kindergarten, thus shorn of healthful individuality and vigour, could never become rooted in English soil.

Passing on from infants and little children to the physical education of girls, let us consider the wants in this respect of the little girl of seven years of age entering upon school life. She is still on a par with boys of her own age in activity and muscular strength. So far their lines of growth have been parallel, and in general conformation, keen relish for exercise, powers of endurance, and muscular development, they are alike. The boy is perhaps on an average a trifle stronger than the girl, his bones a little heavier, but so slightly marked and so inconstant are these differences that anatomists cannot distinguish between the skeleton of a boy and a girl at this age—they speak only of the characteristics of the child—and it is during the second period of childhood (from seven to fourteen), and the period of youth which succeeds to it, that secondary differences of bodily conformation distinctive of sex supervene.

The child of seven, if it has been allowed a reasonable

amount of freedom, has, whether it has passed through the Kindergarten or not, been so constantly on the move, has had so much play involving brisk exercise of all its muscles, that it generally thrives and grows strong in spite of many hindrances to the healthful unfolding and strengthening of its faculties founded on misconception and ignorance, or inherent in the conditions of life of its parents. It has probably not yet ceased to use the left hand almost indifferently with the right, notwithstanding oft repeated reprimands on the awkwardness of so doing. If it has already been confined in a close schoolroom, and made to sit still on an uncomfortable seat or at a desk for several hours a day, the chances are that it throws its flexible body into so many contortions, and indulges in so many antics when school hours are over, that no permanent injury has resulted from long enforced continuance in one position.

Of boys the same may be said all through their school lives excepting only studious, or very delicate, slightly made boys. The cricket matches eagerly looked forward to, practised for, and entered into heart and soul, the rowing on the river, swimming, wrestling, leaping, and the thousand forms of so-called mischief in which boys indulge when let out of school, counterbalance the irksome restraints and the positive injuries of their rough-and-ready school life, in this country at least; and, therefore, in spite of having often little thought bestowed on their school arrangements from the health point of view, they have a chance of growing up strong, vigorous, straight, and capable of physical endurance and exertion.

With girls it is different. From the time of their regular entrance into the schoolroom, they are expected to lay aside all vigorous play, and to be a hoyden or a tomboy is often thought to be the very acme of impropriety in a young schoolgirl. Intellectual training in the better class of schools, dull learning by rote in the inferior ones, takes henceforth the first place in a girl's education, and seldom indeed do we find the physical needs of a growing and delicate organization come in for anything approaching adequate attention either in school or home education. And yet with children generally, and with girls especially, the training of the physical powers should take precedence over the training of the intellectual powers, the latter being incapable of unfolding harmoniously in a stunted or deformed body, however brilliant may be the temporary or one-sided intellectual development of some overstimulated or sickly children.

Let us study first the natural differences between girls and boys in the middle of school life. The difference in strength and solidity of bony structure shadowed forth in early childhood has become accentuated. The spinal column, with its many beautiful arrangements for supporting the weight of the body, and allowing of easy and vigorous movements,* being largely composed of bone, is weaker in girls, and its adjustments, therefore, are thrown more easily out of order. The natural curves of the spine, which develop during childhood, have a tendency to become exaggerated in girls, and persistent stooping and slight lateral deviations are among the commonest departures from the healthy standard met with in girlhood. The chest is less capacious. The pelvis, or irregular

* In children the spine or vertebral column is composed of thirty-three separate bones called vertebræ, jointed together, and placed regularly one above another, similar part to similar part, so as to form the skeleton column. Interposed between the bodies, or thick parts of each pair of vertebræ, is a plate formed of a thickly felted material called fibro-cartilage, elastic and tough like indiarubber. Each body has a ring attached to it behind, which is part of a long bony case, the spinal canal, in which the delicate spinal cord is lodged, and carefully protected from jar or pressure under ordinary circumstances. Projecting from this ring are several little levers of bones called processes, which afford points of attachment for the muscles, and enable them to give motion of the most complex nature to all the parts composing the flexible whole.

bony girdle attached above to the lower part of the spine, below to the lower extremity, is larger in girls than in boys, and the muscular system generally is less well developed.

From the differences which have thus sprung up between girls and boys may be deduced the special indications for physical education of a girl's growing frame.

1. The spine is weaker; therefore it should be less heavily weighted.

2. The chest is less capacious; therefore it ought at least to have no hindrances placed in the way of its expansion, but have perfect freedom to enlarge and develop its normal shape and proportions.

3. The pelvis is larger; therefore the organs contained in it are more apt to suffer displacement either from compression of the soft abdominal wall about the level of the waist, or as a consequence of severe physical strain, whether caused by exercise too prolonged or by exercise too severe in its nature.

4. The muscular system is less well developed; therefore it requires to have the special attention of parents and educators directed towards it, for the purpose of strengthening it and making it fit to sustain the functions of mature life.

Apart from such general duties towards children of both sexes as a regular supply of suitable food, which is as necessary, but not more so, to girls as to boys, and the recognition of the important principle that intellectual training ought, during the years of ordinary school life, that is, up to the age of adolescence, to be subordinated both for boys and for girls to physical and moral training, let us consider one by one the principal things which, from our point of view, require to be modified or reformed in the education of girls.

I. Dress.

Girls' dress cries imperiously for reform. In our country flannel underclothing is a hygienic necessity; it is the best means we possess of guarding against the extremes of temperature to which our shifting climate exposes us. As a rule, boys, after they have passed through the perilous age of bare necks and short petticoats, which sees so many of them sink into the grave, victims of their mothers' ignorance or folly, are clothed from head to foot in flannel or in woollen cloth, unless they have the misfortune to be born to such pinching poverty that anything more than decent covering for the body is looked upon as superfluous. Girls, as a rule, in all classes of society, have only the merest pretence of flannel underclothing, which serves merely to exaggerate the difference of temperature between the exposed and the covered portions of the body. The trunk is indeed generally clothed in merino or flannel, but for the upper half of the chest no underclothing is provided, and half or the whole of the lower extremities are cased in cotton undergarments. The texture of the upper garments is often flimsy, and unsuitable to a climate in which summer clothing is never required for more than a few weeks at a time. And even the insufficient warm clothing which the girl usually wears is lessened on festive occasions, when it is thought quite right to lower a girl's flannel by two or three inches, to allow of her exposing her neck and chest more completely at an evening party in the depth of winter. All this is wrong, is a positive sin against nature and against common sense.

If we want to rear healthy girls, we must protect them against the inclemency of the climate by clothing them in flannel, not by making believe to do so. We must teach them those personal duties to themselves and social duties to others which they and we violate, by recklessly exposing their bodies to the inroads of disease just as much as if they were made to swallow some poisonous draught. Girls should be taught from a very early age that wilfully or carelessly to sow the seeds of illness or weakness in themselves is to sin against their body and to nullify the promise of usefulness to others in which all young creatures should delight. That would be truer education than to teach them the names and dates of all our bloody battles, or the exact order of succession of our English kings. I do not wish to undervalue the teachings of history, and I should be sorry indeed to see girls grow up ignorant of the principal events which have succeeded each other in their own and in other countries; but if one kind of learning must needs be sacrificed to the other, let it not be the one which is indispensable to the raising up of a healthy generation of women.

Another important, commonly overlooked, point in girls' dress is that it should be light and suitably adjusted. A heavy material does not necessarily imply more warmth than one of different make weighing much less. Fine soft serge may be as warm as a coarse heavy one, and merino or cashmere is as warm as velveteen; but the difference in actual weight to be borne is considerable. If to difference of material are added differences in length and cut in a dress, and the presence or absence of heavy flouncing or kilting, giving no uniform warmth to the body, but constituting a drag on the spine of the most pernicious and wearisome description, it needs no anatomist, one would think, to pronounce that the choice and adjustment of a girl's clothing so as to minimize drag and to prevent pressure from being exercised on internal organs or on important masses of muscle, instead of being borne by the bony framework of the body, is a necessary subject of anxious thought to mothers and educators, and that dress may undoubtedly be made one valuable means of physical education.

At the present day it is generally admitted that the spine of girls is weaker than that of boys, and yet they alone of the two have been singled out to wear numerous heavy skirts, sometimes so tight that walking is an unsightly and painful exercise, sometimes, just as blind fashion may dictate, inordinately wide and maintained by hoops at such a distance from the body that currents of cold air circulate with ease between them and the body they cover. It is known that a girl's chest is less capacious than that of a boy, and yet it is the girls who are put into stays and compressed round the waist by bands and strings almost always too tight for comfortable breathing, and which should not by rights be there at all to impede the circulation and alter the shape of the viscera they overlie. We recognize that the muscular system is less well developed in girls than in boys, and yet, as if we wanted to make their muscles waste, girls' clothing is so ill arranged that they cannot even walk without discomfort, and are effectually prevented from deriving much pleasure from exercises of a more vigorous kind, such as rowing and skating,* for which nature has in no way disqualified them, and which, when learnt in early girlhood, are so conducive to robust health and innocent enjoyment.

Girls ought to be first clothed according to correct principles; and, secondly, they ought to be taught those principles. They should know, for instance, why it is wrong for them to have twenty to thirty yards of material put into one dress, even though the money to pay for it may be quite a secondary consideration; why their undergarments should be light and warm enough to enable them to dispense with multitudinous skirts; why no tight strings or bands should fasten round the waist, compressing the lower ribs and important abdominal organs;

---

* Great care is necessary in teaching grown-up women to skate, or even to row, as the consequences of skating tumbles or of over-exertion in rowing may be serious to them; and no violent exercise ought ever to be taken when the pelvic organs are in a state of congestion.

why they should wear no stays, and allow the chest to expand and grow in its natural form, that is to say, to widen and not to become narrower at its lower part. It is not quite enough to say, as a good New England mother once said to her little girl, a friend of mine, when teazed by her to be allowed to wear stays: "Lizzie, if God had made little girls to want the support of stays, He would have put steel casings round them. You can wear stays, if you like, when you are grown up and your own mistress, but as long as you are my little girl, you wear no stays." Girls must be shown what mischief results from compressing the lower part of the chest, and altering its natural shape out of all symmetry and beauty, the impeded growth and displacement of internal parts, the weakening of the muscles of the back, condemned by the use of stays to inactivity, the interference with the orderly course of the circulation of the blood, the general impairment of nutrition and the dwarfing of the physical life, and, through it, of the whole life of the heedless or ill-advised young creature, who seeks to attain through physical deformity to a false ideal of womanly beauty. The Venus de' Medici, of medium stature and perfect proportions, is twenty-seven inches round the waist. How many young women who have grown up in stays, whether they be of medium height or tall, ever attain such healthy development of chest and muscle as a girth of twenty-seven inches at the waist implies!

Again, as to boots. It is not enough for a wise mother to say to a girl: "You are not to wear high-heeled boots, because they are bad for you." That may do for the period of childhood and early girlhood; but once released from authority, of course the girl will follow the prevalent fashion of the day, unless she has been convinced that it is fraught with danger. She must have learnt, if she is by her own free will to eschew high and slanting heeled boots, that they will destroy the natural form of the bones of her foot, and give her in a less degree the deformity of a Chinese lady's foot; that they predispose to painful joint affections, cause permanent contraction of certain muscles of the leg during walking and standing, throw the weight of the body forward, and cause even curvature of the spine to be developed, in order to restore the disturbance of equilibrium caused by withdrawing the heel of the foot from its natural function of helping materially to support the weight of the body. Similarly, a disturbance of equilibrium occurs, followed by its own train of evils, when tight or narrow-soled and ill-cut boots, which destroy the natural arch of the foot, or twist and cramp it, are worn. That boots should be of a quality and texture to keep the feet dry and warm is almost too obvious to need insisting on, were it not that many women choose boots for themselves and their young daughters as if boots existed to make their feet look pretty, and nothing more. The whole question of boots is interesting, and by wearing them at all we lose much valuable service which the foot might render as a tactile and prehensile organ. The foot is undoubtedly capable of bearing a good deal of exposure, and in more temperate climates than our own something might be gained, and much enjoyment afforded, by dispensing with any covering for the foot; but where covering is worn, it should be sufficiently thick and strong to protect the foot from ordinary injuries, and to preserve it from undue extremes of temperature, as well as so fashioned as to allow of a good deal of movement in various directions.

The above brief remarks have, I hope, sufficed to make it evident to all that girls have been grievously sinned against by their educators in the matter of dress, and that it is impossible to carry out any large measure of reform in their physical education without first introducing a little more common sense into the dressing of girls, and casting aside those trammels to free and healthy development of the body which fashion and the folly of mothers have devised.

II. Exercise.

Having cleared the way by first reviewing the question of dress, for what may be called the more positive part of our subject, let us now consider exercise, and see whether the rights of girl children to a free development of their faculties are not here also violated.

Little girls of the working classes are exercised often severely enough. They are less likely to be dragged down by the weight of their skirts; the danger is rather that their garments are both too few for warmth and of unsuitable materials. They are less often cramped by stiff stays than girls of the richer classes, but when they are put into stays, the consequences are in some respects even more disastrous, as the common kinds of stays, which may be bought for a couple of shillings, are worse cut than the more expensive ones; and it is no uncommon thing for such pressure to be exercised by their stays on the growing breasts of young working girls as to make them incapable as mothers of ever giving their children suck.

Little girls of the working classes, if they are not dragged down by heavy skirts, are very commonly weighed down by heavy babies. The practice of making an older child act as nurse to her little brothers and sisters, and carry on her arm (almost invariably the left one) heavy babies, which a girl of the same age in well-to-do families would hardly be allowed to lift from the ground, and of sending out very young or slight, delicate girls into service as nursemaids, as the lightest and most suitable work for them, is the most frequent cause of spinal curvature and its long train of evils in the children of the poor. Boys, when they are made to nurse the baby, and this they have to do as a rule only when there are no sisters old enough to do it—the work is never evenly divided among the boys and girls of a family—are both a little stronger to bear the burden and less conscientious about their little charges than girls are. They run away and cannot be made to give up their lives to the service of the baby as girls often do, a girl sometimes nursing through a large family of brothers and sisters—at least this was so before the days of Schoolboards—now there is less chance of it—and it is one of the most useful services which Schoolboards are rendering to the community, that they are delivering little girls from the thraldom of the baby, and removing one of the most prolific causes of crooked backs in girls. It may be that they are substituting others, but of this more anon.

It has long been known that, if you overload a young horse or other beast of burden, its back bends, and its future serviceableness is impaired; and yet I have known honest, hardworking English mothers who hardly ever took up their babies except to suckle them, and left the entire nursing of them to the eldest little girl of the family, to her physical injury and to the neglect of her schooling. It used to be no rare thing to find the eldest girl in fairly prosperous working men's families unable to read or write like the rest, because she had only had two or three quarters' schooling, having been kept at home to mind the successive babies, of which there was always one from the time she could walk alone until she was sent out into service to earn her own living. Truly it may be said that "Evil is wrought by want of thought, as well as by want of heart," when we reflect that nothing short of compulsory education has sufficed to lift from the shoulders of little girls so heavy a burden; and when we remember that it was their mothers who placed it there, what more convincing proof need we ask of the advisability, nay the absolute necessity, of imparting to women the largest possible measure of useful knowledge, seeing that they contribute so materially by wise household government, or the contrary, to make or to mar the health and usefulness of the rising generation, apart altogether from their own inalienable right to a share in the intellectual banquet of life?

If there happens to be no baby in the family, little girls of the working class are still expected to help actively in household work, at times when boys are generally sent out to amuse themselves, in order, as the mothers often express it, "to get them out of the way." Some kinds of household activity, such as cleaning rooms and boots, washing up, running errands, &c., afford capital exercise to both boys and girls, but it frequently happens that most of the fetching of water and coals is left to the girl, while the stronger boy is playing in the streets. Again, the girl, when she comes home from school, is often set down to needlework, a useful and necessary occupation, I grant, but one which is monotonous in the extreme, wearisome to active little brains, almost always pursued in a stooping posture, and which, as a physical exercise, to use the words of an excellent and judicious teacher of girls,* " may almost be pronounced bad in its very nature." It calls into action a limited number of muscles of the hand and arm only (and it may be remarked that those muscles which are active in sewing get plenty of exercise during school hours), while it hardly calls forth any activity in the muscles of the thumb, which good physical education ought to develop to the utmost, the thumb being that part of the hand which is most essentially human in its characteristics. Knitting, especially in the German way, is far superior to sewing as a manual exercise; and there is much to be said in support of the proposal made by a lady member of one of our provincial Schoolboards, that boys should be taught to knit, as well as girls, as a good and useful manual exercise.

Little girls of the middle and upper classes, whose parents do not look to their labour as a right which is to take precedence of education, exercise, and play, are often, strange to

* Anna C. Brackett, " Education of American Girls," 1874.

say, at a greater disadvantage than even their poorer sisters, when compared with their brothers, in regard to the means afforded to them of physical education and development. They are, as already stated, most unsuitably dressed. Their education is either neglected, on the plea of their brothers' greater needs, if the family purse is small, and they are not allowed, for fear of becoming unfeminine, to make up for the want of good teaching by living in the open air and growing strong of limb, active, observant, enduring, and fearless, or they are immured in school-rooms for many hours of the day, tormented with accomplishments (which they seldom accomplish), and, on pretence of pushing them forward intellectually, and making them the equals of their brothers, they are taught the same lessons without being given the same correctives of over-activity of brain, which their brothers enjoy when they rush out of school wild with exuberance of spirits and eager for fun.

The danger of intellectual forcing of girls is great in our own day, awaking as we are to the educational wants of women. High-schools are growing up in all our large towns for middle-class girls, and girls of the working classes are being slowly but surely gathered into Board schools. There is not much danger that girls' minds will be too well stored, although it is a startling fact that conscientiousness in doing their lessons well is apt to develop uncomfortably early in little girls as compared with little boys. We need not fear that women will become too learned, but we have reason to fear that their intellectual training will be pushed too far at an early age, to the detriment of their physical, and especially of their muscular, development.

Teachers are not all to blame for this. There is in them a natural leaning to exaggerate the importance of the subjects they individually teach, which, however, makes them all the better teachers if it is counterbalanced by similar feeling in all the other teachers in the school, and greater breadth of view in the head-mistress. Too much is demanded of teachers and schoolmistresses by parents and guardians. A girl is expected to have made too great and sustained intellectual efforts by the time she leaves school, and school life is regarded far too much as a time for laying in a stock of intellectual provision for the whole of life. With this feeling abroad, teachers have not fair play. They are driven on by competition to force their pupils' brains; and if they attempt to introduce reforms—to give, for instance, more time and attention to gymnastic exercises for girls—the parents are very apt to tell them that they pay their money for education and not for gymnastics. Quite recently I was amazed to hear fall from the lips of one of the most competent members of the School-board for London the remark, that it was wrong to take away more of the time left to the girls from needlework for physical exercise, because the ratepayers' money was paid after all for intellectual training, and because the girls were made to work at home by their mothers out of school hours, and were sure to get plenty of physical exercise in that way.

I hope I have made it clear to all here present that the exercise which the girls do get at home in working families is not sufficient for their health, at any rate in large towns. Should any still doubt it, a visit to any of our Board schools will convince them that the early grace of childhood has in too many of the girls given place to stooping shoulders, want of accuracy and precision in movement, and awkward, slovenly gait, which may be taken as so many indications that at least that most important branch of physical education, the training of the muscular system, has been insufficient or neglected.

At least a third of a school-girl's life ought to be spent in sleep. Many girls require even more than eight hours' sleep, and it is poor economy of time to stint them of it when this is so. Of the fifteen or sixteen working hours of the day, not more than one-third should be spent in preparing lessons and in class work throughout childhood, and little girls of from seven to ten or eleven years of age ought to have even shorter hours of work. The remaining hours of the day ought to be devoted to taking food and to training the body. The latter, in the natural healthful conditions of country life, would consist of long walks, to which it is easy to bring even young children by regular practice, rambles in search of natural history specimens, climbing hills or mountains, swimming, rowing, skating, riding, lawn tennis, and one or two other really useful modern games, according to the time of year, while for wet days there would be dancing in-doors, battledore and shuttlecock, the old-fashioned games of fives and of cup and ball, which make the hand so nimble and so obedient to the will, and, for all weathers and seasons, looking after and playing with the animals, which go so far to make up the pleasure and usefulness of a country life to children of both sexes. Several hours a day spent in active and varied exercise in country air, with a little sensible supervision and steady discountenancing by the mother of all listlessness and moping, would make every girl strong, supple, surefooted, able to walk and to run, quick and steady of hand and of eye, clear-headed, large-brained, ready, after passing safely through the critical period which leads from childhood to adolescence, to throw herself vigorously into intellectual work, and capable of learning in a year, at sixteen or seventeen years of age, as much as has been compressed into the whole school life of a young girl of average education. There are few kinds of knowledge which cannot be better taken in by the rapidly unfolding brain of the girl entering in upon young womanhood than by the brain of the child; and happily even languages, which are so easily acquired by children, need involve no strain of the immature intellectual faculties, as it is merely the imitative part which it is essential to teach in early childhood.

Thus far I have said nothing about systems of gymnastics or direct methods of physical training for girls, holding it, as I do, to be better and more natural to let them develop in as much freedom from artificial restraints as possible, and being fully persuaded that the various activities of healthy, happy, and cultured country life are in themselves sufficient to train the senses, and to train the muscular system and bring it into subjection to the will, to do which is the essential object of all physical education. If, however, from motives of convenience or necessity, children are brought up in towns, artificial methods of physical training must needs be resorted to, in order to supply the place of natural ones; and it becomes a subject of national importance to study the best gymnastic methods and appliances, to understand clearly the reasons for them, and why it is undesirable to put boys and girls through exactly the same course of gymnastics.

The training of the senses requires no special adaptation for boys or for girls, the element of sex not entering in here at all. To teach the eye to see properly surrounding objects, the ear to hear and discriminate sounds discordant or harmonious, and gradually to educate it up to a perception of the beauties first of simple melody and later on of more complicated musical combinations; to teach the palate to choose and to enjoy harmless, in preference to harmful, food and drink; to train, in short, all the senses to be keen and quick in action, and faithful ministers interposed between the soul and the outer world, is the office of the educator of the youth of both sexes, and need not now occupy us, who have met to consider physical education in its special bearing on girls.

Where children grow up in the freedom of country life, it is needless to prescribe minutely how far a boy may run or how high he may climb in excess of a girl, and it is never necessary to tell a big girl that she must not play at cricket with the youths of the neighbourhood. Girls feel no pleasure in taking more physical exercise than their frame is fitted for, any more than a healthy palate prompts to gluttony or excess. There are natural adjustments and instincts of propriety which may safely be trusted more than they are to choose what is really befitting to girls and boys. But if children are taken out of their natural medium, country life, and bred in cities, with artificial gymnastics to develop and strengthen their muscles, instead of the manifold activities of country life, then it becomes necessary to study carefully and to follow faithfully the differences which sex has implanted in boys and girls, and it behoves us to beware that we respect in our systems of physical education the laws of development of either sex.

We have then to consider that, from their general conformation and the special maternal functions for which nature is slowly and silently fashioning them, gymnastic exercises for girls must be less violent, perhaps more frequent, but certainly less prolonged, than those designed for boys. In later girlhood girls may even require occasional short intermittences on account of temporary weakness or trifling indispositions, whence it is obvious that it is most consistent with delicacy and propriety that the gymnastic exercises of girls should be performed under the direction of thoroughly qualified and efficient women teachers, who can best estimate the varying physical capacity of the developing girl, and who can, as a matter of course, question her pupils on health subjects which cannot with any propriety be discussed by a man with young girls. Again, into the question of gymnastics for girls the consideration of the relatively large size of their pelvis, the position of the organs contained in it, and their liability to congestion, displacement and strain in consequence of ill-directed gymnastic exercise, or still more pernicious rivalry between girls of unequal physical power, enters largely. In short, the gymnastic training of girls involves so many questions of detail and of compromise between the general and the particular that I fail to see how any one but a woman, qualified for the work by nature and by the best and most thorough training, can carry it out satisfactorily. A woman also can far more efficiently than a man train young women teachers, appreciating, as she only can do, the weariness and actual hard work that it is to them, with their consolidated frames and disobedient muscles, to master exercises which are mere child's play to supple young girls.

So far Ling's exercises, the so-called Swedish gymnastics, have been found most suitable for girls; but I confess I look forward to a time when some woman of genius shall, with all the learning of the schools at her command, joined to her own special feminine instinct, have given us something even better and more completely adapted to the requirements of girls than Ling's system of gymnastics.

In all systems of gymnastics—and perhaps this is more necessary for girls than for boys, as women's lives are spent more at home, and manual dexterity is of even more moment to them than to men, on account of the variety of work for which handiness is demanded in a household, although, alas! it is often demanded in vain—training of the hand ought to hold a prominent place.

The left hand especially requires to be reinstated in its natural position of equal co-operation with the right from which centuries of misdirected educational efforts have driven it. Instead of striving to prevent a child from making use of its left hand, and forcing it to use almost exclusively the right, our endeavour should be to make it equally expert with both hands, not alone for the sake of the increased capacity for all kinds of manual work thus gained, but also as a means of indirectly developing the right or corresponding half of the brain, on which muscular activity reacts as a powerful stimulus. Education has taken a direction so entirely false in regard to the left hand that it has created a wholly artificial necessity for special left-hand gymnastics, to counteract not only actual wrong teaching but inherited wrong tendencies; for the very slight preference which perhaps a small majority of infants give to the right hand over the left would never, without the injudicious fostering of parents, have resulted in that maiming of the race which righthandedness implies. That the disability is an artificial and not a natural one is proved by the fact that energetic individuals once as righthanded as their fellows do sometimes teach themselves to become ambidexter when circumstances make it desirable or necessary; and that they should be able to do so is the less to be wondered at when we reflect there has been in our own day such a prodigy as an artist of considerable merit, born without hands, who painted his pictures with his feet, which long use had rendered as deft as other people's hands.

In estimating the advantages girls would derive from a rational system of physical education, it is often overlooked that, apart from the general advantage to all human beings of well-developed muscles, and the importance of muscular exercise as a promoter of the venous circulation, together with its strengthening and steadying influence on the nervous system, muscular exercise retards the advent of puberty by directing an abundant supply of blood to the active muscles, whereas muscular inactivity favours congestion of internal organs, precocious sexual development, with all its long train of physical and moral evils, and that hydra-headed parent of female ailments in civilized communities, instability of the nervous system, or disturbed equilibrium of the motor and sensory divisions.

The special duties of women make large calls on muscular strength; and if in childhood the opportunity afforded of developing it is missed, how can these claims be met? Is it not pitiable to see yearly thousands of mothers break down under the burden of maternity borne for the first or second time, while it is no exaggeration to say that not twenty per cent of English mothers belonging to the upper classes of society are physically capable of carrying about in their arms their own babies, but must perforce make them over to the care of strangers? Is it too much to say of women that they "need strong arms that can cradle a healthy child and hold it crowing in the air, backs that will not break under the burden of household cares, a frame that is not exhausted and weakened by the round of daily duties?"*

When I look round among the women whose family history is known to me, and with whose maternal experiences professional acquaintanceship has made me familiar, I find that all those who have safely and easily passed through the crises of motherhood without impairment of general health are muscularly well developed; most of them led as children a free outdoor country life; and a large proportion were their brothers' playmates and comrades in girlhood in all their active sports. This entirely coincides with medical experience generally, for the almost incredible expenditure of muscular force which women have to sustain in a single day during the exercise of their most laborious maternal function, cannot fail to overdraw, if it does not exhaust, the strength and powers of endurance of those women who, as one of our well-known obstetricians has aptly put it, "have never done a hard day's work in their lives before."

I am content to rest my claim for the physical education of girls on their universally recognized right to become in fulness of time wives and mothers; for if it be once admitted that it is due to girls to spare no pains to make them strong for the performance of their special womanly duties, we need ask for no more. Girls of the physical calibre which will make them the strong mothers of a strong race are sure to have such a foun-

* Dr. Elizabeth Blackwell, "Lectures on the Laws of Life," 1871.

dation of health and strength, such firmness of muscle, such well-strung nerves, such well-developed brains (for it must not be forgotten that the size and quality of the brain is largely influenced by the muscular development of the body), that they will be able to accomplish without strain a very large amount of intellectual work; able, in fact, to do any kind of intellectual work which they deliberately elect to do. And we shall be no more assailed with pitiful tales of girls crushed under the weight of competitive examinations, of over-active brains in feeble bodies, giving way for years or for life. We shall hear no more, in short, of those disgraceful breakdowns of health on the threshold of adult life which bring such discredit on the movement for the higher education of women, although they are by no means confined to the female sex.* For a girl to break down under pressure of intellectual work is, I contend, a disgrace to those who have been entrusted with her early training, no less than a discredit to herself, and a dishonour to the woman's cause; and it is high time to raise our voices in strong protest against such waste of precious young human life, such violation of physiological laws, and such criminal ignorance of the conditions and requirements of healthy development in women.

* In the first mixed class of anatomy at the College of Surgeons, Edinburgh, in 1870, keen competition for the prize took place between the male and female students, and the teachers still speak with wonder of the great amount of earnest work accomplished by all during the session. The ladies gave the best average; a lady came in for the second place, and three out of the seven took honours; but a gentleman took the first prize. He, however, went up immediately afterwards for an examination in anatomy before the College of Surgeons of England and failed ignominiously. So utterly had he broken down physically and mentally that, as he himself expressed it, his brain whirled, and he was unable to name correctly even the two bones of the forearm; and it was many months before he recovered. Yet the ladies were all mentally and physically stronger at the end than they were at the beginning of the session.

THE HAPPINESS OF CHILDHOOD.

By ANNA BUCKLAND.

There seems to be a widespread feeling that the present generation, with all its rich stores inherited from the past, and all its own gains in the present, has yet failed in the attainment of happiness. Due allowance must, of course, be made, for the tendency of some imaginations at all times to dwell on the dark side of things; and we must also reckon for the existence in every age of "melancholy philosophers," who "love to sit down and rail against the world;" but beyond the vein of sadness, which has its place in every age, there is at the present time a too general expression of disappointment with life and its results for us to doubt that a sense of unhappiness is common; and the cry for light and good has an intensity which carries the conviction that it is also real. Yet the world has not grown old, nor have the conditions of human existence greatly changed. All the sources of human happiness—God, Love, Duty, Nature, are as full and deep as ever, as fresh and pure and unexhausted.

> "For while a youth is lost in soaring thought,
> And while a maid grows sweet and beautiful,
> And while a springtide coming lights the earth,
> And while a child, and while a flower is born,
> And while one wrong cries for redress and finds
> A soul to answer,——Still the World is young."

The unhappiness of the present generation does not lie

in the decay of those sources from which happiness is derived; but in the want of accord between the race of to-day, and the world above and around them. They turn from the springs of joy, because these no longer refresh and satisfy them. They have lost the power of receiving and assimilating what once gave happiness to life, and made it beautiful and precious. It is sometimes suggested that the human race has made in the present century such progress that it has outgrown the power of enjoyment; the aims of the present generation are so high that life cannot satisfy them; their knowledge of human nature is so enlarged, their sympathies so quickened, that happiness is no longer possible, except as a selfish dream.

Yet the greatest men the world has ever seen, the men of highest aims, of largest knowledge of human nature, and of keenest, tenderest sympathy, have shown a simple gladness of heart, and a power of entering into all the life of the world, and of receiving happiness from all its various sources. And this must be so, for the greater is the nature of the man, the larger is his sphere of life; his outlook is wider, and he fearlessly includes all things within it; it is by his very many-sidedness that he is capable of receiving a larger measure of happiness from a greater variety of sources. It is not greatness, but narrowness, which is the cause of unhappiness; and it is not the "progress" or "growth" of the present generation, which is the occasion of its vein of sadness. Growth is not the hasty running up in a single line; and progress is not advance only in one direction. The growth of the individual is the equal and constantly increasing development of every faculty; and the progress of the race is when "the whole world grows like the few." We do not need to lower our aims, nor to become ignorant and callous in order to be happy; but we need rather to aim at nothing short of perfecting the ideal of humanity; and to strive to keep in active exercise every faculty of soul, and mind, and heart. We can only outgrow happiness when one part of our complex nature outgrows another. In a true, complete growth, happiness rises ever before us, extending onwards into a divine fulness, and into the long vista of immortality.

Happiness begins with life; the little gentle murmurs of contentment are contemporary with the tears and cries; and very soon the sunny smiles and joyful laugh of childhood far out-number the signals of distress. It now rests with those who have the care and training of the little one in their hands to provide for him the means of happiness, and to guard and cultivate those faculties by which he is able to derive pleasure from all its pure and unexhausted sources.

But here come in two or three ideas, which prevent parents and teachers from making the happiness of children a direct aim of their guardianship and training. First, there is the old superstitious *fear* of happiness; the dread that the hearty enjoyment of the blessings of life will provoke the displeasure of some mysterious power which can be thus moved to deprive us of them. Then there is a feeling, that if children are made too happy in this world, they will learn to rest satisfied with it, and have no aspirations beyond an earthly life. Again, the notion has become common, that happiness is very unheroic, incompatible with depth of earnestness and intense feeling. And lastly, there is a general idea that all children are naturally so full of happiness that we need not seek it for them in any scheme of education or training; what we have to do is to seek their "*good*," and they may be left to find happiness for themselves.

It is certainly time that we got rid of the first of these ideas; for if we believe, with Fröbel, that each little child is a thought of God, we must also believe that he was sent into a world prepared for him,—a world in harmony with his nature;—and that, therefore, the smile of God must rest on the little child, who heartily and freely delights in the rich provision made for his happiness.

And can we believe, that by allowing a child to be miserable in this world we are leading him to love God, its Creator, and raising any aspiration which would make the child desire to enter another world of nearer access to God? Unhappiness may cause a distaste for this life; but that is not an aspiration after a higher life; it is only a desire for a change; which would be sufficiently satisfied by other conditions of earthly life, without the same drawbacks, even if the state were a lower one. It is rather by a spring-time of happiness that the little child learns to love God, the Maker of the world in which he finds himself, and to believe in and desire an after world of richer blessedness, and of more joyful nearness to the Father of all mercies.

And need we fear that a happy childhood lays the foundation of an unheroic character in after life? Idleness and self-indulgence will do this; but not happiness. It is grief, which is too often selfish, and discontent and murmuring, which shut up sympathy. A miserable childhood, with its self-engrossment, is not the foundation of large-hearted, self-sacrificing love in later life; nor are weariness and disappointment in childhood a preparation for hopeful work in the ripe season of maturity.

So far from our being relieved from all responsibility in regard to the happiness of children—because they will be sure to make themselves happy in some way—the fact is, that at no period of our lives are we anything like so susceptible of sorrow as in childhood. More tears are shed in childhood than at any other time; and this is not merely for the reason that little eyes fill more readily; childhood's tears are not "idle tears" because the cause of sorrow seems to us so trifling; they "rise in the heart," as well as "gather to the eyes;" and the heart-ache is as sore as that caused by what we call our greater trials. There is no stage of life in which happiness is so dependent on things outside of ourselves as in childhood. In after years, when life is more in our own hands, we are generally, more or less, the makers of our own happiness; but in helpless childhood—when we look to others for everything, when every delicate fibre of the being clings to something outside of itself, when all the circumstances and direction of life, the work, the play, the health, all the soothing and cheering influences, are in the hands of others—it is clear that the risk to happiness is very great.

There is then every reason why we should fearlessly and earnestly make the happiness of children a part of our purpose and aim in all our plans for them of education, training, or general life.

A few suggestions may be useful in regard to some of the conditions on which the happiness of childhood depends; and these we may divide under two heads—those which must enter into schemes of education and training; and those which belong to the personal influence of individuals.

The first essentials of any plan of education which shall result in the happiness of the child are, that the system should include means for the equal development and growth of every faculty of the child; and that these should be planned in strict accordance with the natural laws of a child's being. Every Kindergarten teacher knows that these two principles are the foundation of Fröbel's system, and that the Kindergarten is a complete series of exercises for every faculty of the child, under which each petal of the little human flower is unfolded in strict accordance with natural laws. That the result should be happiness, we need only enter a Kindergarten to prove, or ask a little child thus educated which are the happiest hours of the day. It is in fact simply "Nature's holy plan;" and it "every flower enjoys the air it breathes," and it is with a thrill of pleasure that "the budding twigs spread out their fan," it may well be our faith that the unfolding and growth of the child's more sensitive nature are attended by the most delightful consciousness of happiness. But on the other hand, have we not also "reason to lament what man has made of man?" For it is by a system of training which unduly stimulates certain faculties, and utterly neglects others, that we have produced the weariness and feverish restlessness which are the misery of the present generation. What thousands of bright little eyes have been made to weep over the constant taxes on the tired memory; and what thousands of childish sighs have arisen over painful efforts to use the overstrained reason; while at the same time the imagination has been craving for its food, and the little hands and feet are restless with suppressed activity. Even a child becomes early conscious of a sense of dissatisfaction under a culture which makes no appeal to the soul, provides no exercise for the imagination, has nothing in it to touch the heart, and gives no employment or teaching to the busy fingers; and as he becomes older the poverty of such an existence is painfully present to him.

It is to a wider scheme of education, having for its aim not merely self-preservation and a high condition of physical well-being—but the fuller realization of the Divine ideal in each human being that we must look for the renewal in the next generation of the power of living " a life worth living," a fresh many-sided life of happiness and hope.

A second condition essential to the happiness of childhood is *Freedom*. It is a common cry, that children have too much liberty in the present day; and if the sacred name of liberty is used here for license to follow every desire the assertion may be true. But this is not freedom; and it is a fact, that while license is permitted, freedom is checked and suppressed.

Freedom is only the living out of our true real life—the being what we really are; it is the dwelling under the wide arch of Heaven, with space for abundant natural growth, and the unfettered exercise of every faculty and activity.

We grant, that the nations of the world which enjoyed in their infancy the largest measure of freedom have made the soundest progress, that they have become the most intelligent and moral, and have shown the strictest regard for law. Yet we often fear to let children alone to live out their true natural life, but make it a duty to be constantly thwarting their wishes and checking their impulses; driving them by force in one direction, and holding them back with a strong hand from another, until they become miserable through despondency and irritability. We want more faith in nature and in God; for if we believe that each little child is a thought of God, and that all the laws of its being are divine in their origin, we may well suspect that these are often more true in their promptings than are our plans and notions.

The ordinary restraints placed upon the freedom of a child arise usually from three causes. They are often a part of an artificial system of education, which has settled how the child is to be trained and taught, without any regard to the natural laws of a child's development. The system has perhaps been handed down from the ignorance of the past, and is therefore continued without thought by later generations. There is a notion that what we had to endure ourselves we ought to make the next generation endure. We have turned out so well, we cannot do better than put our children under the same yoke. Or the artificial system is founded on the one idea that happens to be the reigning tendency of the day; and to the preponderating influence of this everything else gives way; so that the free growth of the child is sacrificed to the tyranny of a single thought. The freedom of childhood is again often interfered with by the fact that the parent or teacher has formed a certain ideal, which he holds to be the only model type of childhood. To this one narrow pattern he strives to conform children of utterly contrary characters and natures; so that their early years are passed in constant truggle or in weak despair. All the while the character and capabilities receive no culture. There is a good illustration of the tyranny of a fixed, narrow ideal over a child's life, and of the misery produced by it, in one of Robert Buchanan's "Village Idylls," where an old Scotch shepherd and his wife, whose sole ideal of highest manhood is a minister of the Kirk, strive in vain to train up a poet son in accordance with this ideal. And how many a gifted boy and girl, full of God-given faculties of a particular kind, have had their childhood embittered by attempts to crush the life out of the faculties they had, and to force others they did not possess!

Personal tyranny is another great check on the freedom which is essential to the happiness of a child. The arbitrary will of the parent, or teacher, is exerted to domineer over the will of the child, and this is sometimes done in the belief that it is by this means that a child learns respect and obedience. The child is therefore contradicted without being allowed an answer; no attention is paid to his wishes; he is constantly thwarted in his intentions; and his impulses and tastes are roughly repressed. Even his innocent fancies and feelings are set on one side, and his activities are made to bend under the will of another. But arbitrary rule does not, in itself, inspire respect. True respect is founded on admiration and confidence; and these are only called forth by character and conduct. Children soon see through all paltry attempts to inspire respect by self-assertion and tyranny; and they do not learn true obedience by being forced for a few years to bend to another will, which is exerted only for the sake of over-mastering theirs. "It is good for a man to bear the yoke in his youth," but that is the yoke of *law*, and not of one will domineering over another.

While freedom is essential to the happiness of childhood obedience to law is not less so. Children cannot be taught too early to pay the strictest regard to natural and moral laws; for they are the principles by which we live in harmony with the world in which we dwell, and when this harmony is in any way disturbed, suffering and discord are the unavoidable results. This habit of strict regard to law is not only necessary to the happiness of childhood, but it is the only safeguard against disappointment with life and its results in later years. So little are children taught to live in accordance with law, that they are constantly expecting the good to come, when the law that produces it is set aside, while they resent the evil, which is the natural result of a broken law. In fact, many children are taught not only to believe in, but to expect, miracles with much more certainty than they are led to see the constant, faithful working of God's laws, and the necessity of obedience to them.

In leading children to live in accordance with law, the teaching at first need only be very simple. A little child feels that he is in a world he knows nothing about, and he naturally looks to those who have been longer in it to help him to understand it. At first he has to do with so small a part of the world, and his relations to it are so simple, that the teaching will not be complicated nor over full. The Kindergarten introduces him to one object at a time; and as he learns by degrees the properties of things, and the laws which govern them, it is easy to show him the necessity of obedience to these in his own actions in regard to them. From this he passes on to see the wisdom of God in all these things, and the perfect harmony which subsists between himself and the world around him.

When he acquires the sense that all things around him are ruled according to wise and constant laws ordained by God, his Father, he will lose that blind terror of the unknown and unnatural which is one of the great miseries of childhood. How many a little child's life has been made unhappy by the feeling of insecurity, and the dread of the power of malignant, mysterious agencies.

A habit of obedience to law cannot be acquired, except by the assurance, that the law is constant; and it is, therefore, better not to allow little children to hear of things which are exceptions to the ordinary rule of nature. They need to have the sense of constancy firmly established in their minds before they are made acquainted with those phenomena which result from rare occurrences. And yet it is with these that children are often first made familiar. Many a child has been taught to expect the immediate destruction of the world before he has been told anything of the goodness, constancy and beauty of its wonderful fulness of life. And many a little one has had his happiness broken by the daily expectation of earthquakes, fires, mad dogs, robberies and monsters, before he has learnt that these are unusual occurrences. Even those predictions of terrible storms and sensational weather should be kept from little children, for we cannot tell how these may distress them. A visiting teacher in a preparatory school for little boys happened to mention last summer the prediction that we were to have three days of darkness. This so laid hold of the imagination of one poor little fellow, that on going to bed at night he was heard saying to his companion—"Well this *has* been a miserable day." And a few years ago, when it was predicted that the tail of a comet would destroy the earth, one little child is said to have died from the terror of expecting it.

The first step of the little child will be simple obedience to law, and trust in its constancy; and the result will be the avoidance of suffering and terror; but as the child comes more and more into relation with others, and begins to look up in love to his Father in heaven, obedience to law becomes in him the sense of duty, and his whole moral nature is raised, as he feels love and duty to be the springs of obedience. Then he knows something of that deep happiness which attends duty founded in love, even when the action involves self-denial; and obedience to every law is now in itself a delight, as he recognizes God to be the author of all that divine harmony, by which—

"The very stars are kept from wrong,
And the most ancient Heavens are fresh and strong."

The culture of admiration is another important means of promoting the happiness of childhood. Admiration is essential to all our best life, and is the source of our deepest, sweetest happiness. It is most closely associated with reverence, love and worship. Admiration is cultivated by the training of the æsthetic faculty, and associating with this the observation and perception of beauty wherever it exists, in nature, art, and human character. All education must be one-sided, and all growth deformity if the existence and importance of the æsthetic faculty are ignored, and no provision made for its training and development.

In Fröbel's wide and deeply thought-out scheme we find a variety of means by which, from the earliest years, this faculty receives its due culture.

In the lessons on colour and form the eye of the little child is drawn to beauty of hue and outline; he learns from pictures, and by his own drawing and modelling, the charm of art; in the various objects of nature presented to him he is taught to notice the variety of loveliness and perfection in the works of God; his ear is trained by music and song and rhythmic exercises to delight in sound and in harmony; and by the "use of stories in the Kindergarten" the child is introduced to the great world of the ideal in human character and life. Under this careful training the power of admiration is kept in constant exercise, and the happiness which children through this enjoy only a Kindergarten teacher knows.

It is to this early training that we look with hope for a wider, truer culture of the æsthetic faculty in later life, when the lines started in the Kindergarten are carried on into the study of art and literature. And then the fastidious taste for a particular style, or the false fancy for an exceptional type of character, or single phase of sentiment, will be exchanged for a delight in all the infinitely varied beauty of the whole world of nature and of art; and the full recognition of every sweet and noble element which has a place in God's ideal of man.

The careful training of the Kindergarten teaches children to recognize and delight in the *bits* of beauty in things otherwise imperfect or homely. And this quickness of eye for all that is beautiful and good does not only greatly increase the happiness which is derived from the outward world, but it quickens also the inward eye, to detect broken lights of the divine beauty, shining amongst what is common-place and evil in human character. Here is ground again for the deep joy of undying love, for love is joined with hope, and can suffer long, yet still work on, trusting in the final triumph of good.

From admiration we pass naturally to love as another essential to the happiness of childhood. And here we reach the harmony between man and the world above and around him, without which life is full of discord, misery and despair. Love begins with life, and all love, instinctive love, and gratitude, are a joy to the child; but love founded on admiration, and the satisfying of the ideal, is not reached at once; it is the result of previous steps. It has to do, therefore, with those conditions of happiness which must enter into the scheme of education and training. But through these a little child may be led to find the love of God a source of deepest, sweetest happiness. "We needs must love the highest when we see it;" but the eye needs some preparation before we can see the highest; there are steps in the ascent, and we must be careful, too, to guard against clouds and darkness intervening. Let the thought of God be first associated in the mind of a child with all the good gifts and blessings of life, but not with its catastrophes and terrors. The attempt to impress a child with an idea of the greatness of God from this side produces a wrong conception, because a child cannot associate love with anything but gentleness and tenderness. Thus a little child was told, that the thunder was the voice of God, and this at once produced the remark, "Then I don't like God at all, and never shall." Too often the representation of God made to little children has been such as to produce fear and misery, rather than love and happiness; and many a tender little heart has been filled with self-reproachful grief, because it could not love the object represented as claiming its best affections. There is, of course, a sense in which suffering is the very act of love; but this is a hard lesson, and the tender nature of a little child cannot at first receive it. The more, however, the little child learns to love God in the brightness and happiness of life, the better he will be prepared to still trust and love in the darkness and the storm.

It is unnecessary to enter here on the general subject of religious teaching; but in order that religion may be the happiness of childhood, two things are necessary in regard to it. The teaching must be personal and intelligible. All that makes God known, as the Divine Father, his works, his dealings with man in past ages, and the manifestation of himself in Christ, the Saviour and lover of little children, a child can lay hold of and live by; and unless the religious teaching lead to the personal adoration and love of the Most High, and to trust and obedience, it can be no joy or support to the child. The learning by heart of abstract theology, in whatever way put forth, or of words expressing feelings a child does not experience, can only be dark and wearisome; for a child learns through the imagination and the heart; he can see and love long before he can understand.

God only teaches what the mind can receive; Christ, the Great Teacher, reserved the most important truth until his disciples could receive it; but the minds of little children are often loaded with a mass of unintelligible religious teaching, beneath which they sink oppressed and discouraged. It is this forcing of everything at once upon a child, before he can grasp it, that often makes religious teaching a misery rather than a joy. It is sometimes held to be a duty to teach advanced religious truth to children, so that what they have learnt in childhood may be their support in later years; but unintelligible teaching cannot be a preparation for later experience and needs. It either passes from the mind altogether, or it creates false and grotesque conceptions of solemn things. There is no real need to prepare in childhood for the wants of after life. The best foundation is to teach the child what he can receive and assimilate at the time, that which shall be his life, and strength, and happiness in childhood. There is plenty of religious teaching in the world suited to advanced intelligence, and we may trust that all good seed will be provided with the needful means for its aftergrowth and fuller development. That religion may be a source of happiness in childhood, let us think of the child and not of the man.

An important part of training, as regards the happiness of children, is in self-denial and love to others. Even a child feels the misery of selfishness, and there is scarcely a more unhappy sight than a little creature spoilt by indulgence, and full of itself. The very means taken to make children happy may easily become a cause of misery, if the great object of the loving parent is to satisfy every desire of the child, to give all, and demand nothing in return. The self-engrossment and weary satiety that are a part of the unhappiness of the present generation, have been produced by the too anxious devotion of parents to the physical well-being of their children, and the supplying them with a super-abundance of objective pleasures.

A large family will supply naturally a good deal of the training needed for love and self-denial; but even here it very often happens that while this has been supplied to the elder ones by the claims upon their kindness and care by the little ones, the younger children themselves grow up in thorough selfishness. With an only child the case is still worse. Children need companionship with those of their own age and standing; they need to belong to a community of equals, in order that they may learn sympathy, love, self-repression and harmony of action. Those who know the happy life of the Kindergarten will readily grant its immense influence over children in giving them this kind of training. The spirit of love which prevades every part of Fröbel's system is shown most strongly in the means for training children in thoughtfulness for each other, in unselfish generosity, and in the sense of the brotherhood of humanity and its union, through combined action.

The exercise of compassion and sympathy, joined with active kindness, is always a joy to children; if no attempts are made to force or overstrain the feeling. There is a God given callousness in childhood to the deeper sorrows of life, and we must in no way seek to break this up. The feelings of children can only be trained through the sorrows they can realize and understand. Many a little child has heard without a pang of feeling of terrible accidents and losses of human life, and has yet smudged with heart-felt tears the page in "Original Poems" about "the little bird who built a warm nest in a tree," and was robbed of its young by some boys who were "wicked and rude." The sympathy of children with the oppression of the small and the weak is readier than with the sufferings of men. The story is very characteristic, of the little boy to whom his Mama showed a picture of Daniel in the lions' den. The child sighed and looked much distressed, whereupon his mother hastened to assure him that Daniel was such a good man that God did not let the lions hurt him. "Oh," replied the little fellow, "I was not thinking of that; but what I was afraid of was that those big lions were going to eat all of him themselves, and that they would not give that poor little lion down in the corner any of him."

It is through the little troubles which grieve childish hearts that children learn pity and sympathy. The real feeling called forth by the little bird fallen from its nest and mother's care is an actual development in tenderness; and the gentle treatment of the pet kitten is a real exercise of kindness; and these, if we will only wait till the right time comes, will blossom into genuine philanthropy. The attempt to force and overstrain the feelings of children by those stories of crime and wretchedness which are now so often placed in children's hands is attended by great danger. It is a shock to the simple faith and happy innocence of childhood, and seems to produce in the end a morbid taste for sensational fiction, accompanied by a hardened indifference to real sin and suffering.

It seems scarcely necessary to say that plenty of employment, work, and play is a necessity to the happiness of childhood. The plaintive little cry, "What shall I do? I want something to do," shows a state of fretful dulness that demands immediate attention. Children require help in finding something to do, and to send a child away with an exhortation against idleness, and the command to find some employment, is no better than the Egyptian taskmasters, who said to the Israelites, "Ye are idle, ye are idle," and sent them to make bricks without any straw. A child must be provided with materials for work, and also for play, and he must be taught how to use them. The exercise of invention and construction is a great delight to a child; but both need training, and often help and suggestion. Invention is often slow, and needs quickening, and the little fingers need practice in dexterity, so that the result may give pleasure and satisfaction to the worker. Here, again, the wonderful thought and ingenuity of Fröbel have provided in the Kindergarten a training in work which makes it a constant source of happiness to the child.

But children also need help and suggestion for their play. Play is, as Fröbel saw, the instinctive life of the child expressing itself in action; and he provides for this joyful activity a number of games in which the mind of the child finds pleasure, and the activity is regulated and harmonized, without in any degree suppressing it. The natural plays of children most frequently represent scenes of real life; but a child's experience and knowledge of life is very narrow, and children often weary of repeating the same scenes. In the games of the Kindergarten they are supplied with a large number of dramatic representations of occupations and scenes taken from a variety of different phases of life, such as they could not become acquainted with in their limited experience.

Toys, which are "not too bright and good for human nature's daily food," contribute largely to the happiness of childhood; but even simple toys must not be supplied in such abundance as to produce satiety. Nothing can be worse for a child than to have the toys which he has carelessly broken, or thrown aside, constantly replaced by new ones.

Good toys, which are to make children happy for many a day, must either be such as lay hold of the imagination and the heart, or they must give exercise to a child's activities. We may generally judge what toys answer these ends by the place which certain toys have long held in the estimation of children. Generations of babies have hugged and loved little, white woolly "bow-wows," with black bead eyes and squeaky fore-grounds; and the little boy of to-day believes in his straight-legged, spotted horse, with its furry mane and tail, and cares for its stabling and good treatment with as much faith and love as his father and grandfather had for the same horses in their time; while the little mothers of the nursery still wash and dress and pet their dolls with the same loving tenderness as their mothers and grandmothers bestowed upon the wooden babies of their childhood. Other old toys, the Noah's Ark, the Farmyard, and the Doll's House, keep their places in the regard of children, through the power they have of engaging the imagination. Amongst toys which exercise a child's activity the box of bricks is always a deserved favourite, and does not weary, from its capability of being used in so many different ways. Some new toys of this class have lately been introduced, which give much happiness to children. Amongst these is the little kitchen-stove, in which tiny real dinners can be cooked, and fairy cakes and pies baked. There are also washing-tubs, pails, and mangles, by which busy little washerwomen can get up dolls' clothes in first-rate style; as well as milk-pans, churns, and stamps for making real butter. The box of gardening tools must not be forgotten. A little garden is a constant source of healthy delight to every child. It was part of Fröbel's plan that every child should grow up as much as possible under the influences of nature, and learn her lessons from herself; and the original Kindergartens were held in summer in an open space of ground shaded by trees. Each child had a little piece of ground given to him, where he sowed seeds, and watched the process of their growth, and dug and raked the earth; and gardening formed a part of the Kindergarten occupations. The uncertainty of our climate makes it difficult for Kindergarten teachers to carry out this part of the system in England; but as Fröbel's system is better understood, and when those who have themselves been trained in it become the fathers and mothers of the coming race, care will be taken that the home supplies what the Kindergarten may not be able to accomplish.

It was also a part of Fröbel's plan to have pet animals kept for the children in the Kindergarten to care for and look after. The influence of pet animals has been already referred to as promoting gentleness and tenderness of feeling; but besides these good results, there is great delight in the mutual affection that springs up between children and their pets; and there is great pleasure in attending to the wants of animals, and in watching their habits. The clever little dog, the playful kitten, the pretty rabbits, the gentle dove, the hen and her soft little brood, are unfailing sources of happiness in childhood.

The happiness of children does not entirely depend on conditions belonging to education and training; it is also greatly promoted or checked by the influence of persons around them. It is not enough to provide the essentials of happiness; we must be careful also that we do not destroy the effect of these by our own manner and tone. The special checks to the happiness of children arising from those around them are, irritability, gloom, coldness, and want of sympathy.

Many a well-intentioned parent has made his children miserable, in order that he may indulge his own irritability. The constant fault-finding, the perpetual worrying of children about trifles, seldom spring from any desire for their real improvement; but it affords a convenient outlet for irritability, because children are obliged to take and bear what grown-up persons would resent and put down. Harsh words, severe condemnation of little things, refusals of innocent requests, snubbing and contradicting, wear the hearts and spirits of the little ones until they become in their turn as peevish and miserable as those who have made them so.

Children need to live in the atmosphere of cheerfulness. Their sensitive and delicate natures are far more susceptible to surrounding influences than ours, and they readily take their tone from the persons with whom they live. They are soon cast down by a gloomy parent, teacher, or nurse, whereas they revive like little flowers, and hold up their drooping heads in the presence of a sunny spirit. If we would, as Fröbel urges, "live for our children," we must cast aside our irritability and gloom, and show them at all times the sweetness and light of a loving and bright spirit. And the effort to do this is like mercy " twice blest ; it blesses him that gives, and him that takes."

Children also need warmth, as well as light. They understand but little of the deep love which by self-sacrifice and constant thought seeks their good in all the arrangements of their lives. Many things which a kind and wise parent orders for his children, are not perceived by the children themselves, and much of the conduct of a teacher is misunderstood by his younger pupils ; it is necessary, therefore, to give to children the assurance of love, not only in well-meant deeds, but in the little marks of tenderness and affection, shown by words and caresses. These are the natural expression of a little child's love, and he looks for these in return, and is chilled and repelled by coldness of manner, even where there may be a depth of real love existing in the heart.

Many children suffer very much in childhood from the want of sympathy in those around them. They see that they are misunderstood and misjudged, and yet they cannot explain themselves, or express their real feelings, because they know that if they were to do this older persons would not feel with them. We must not forget that children live in quite another world from ours; but it is one in which we ourselves have once dwelt. It is possible to us, therefore, to look at things from their point of view, although they cannot see things from ours. We have stood where they now stand, and we must strive to become again as little children, to see with their eyes and feel with their hearts ; we must seek to remember what were once our great interests in life, what we chiefly prized, what were our loves, our joys, our griefs, our ignorance, and our fears.

And we may gain help also in the endeavour to sympathize more with children by studying the writings of Fröbel. His long and patient observation of child nature gives to his writings on this subject the trustworthiness of scientific conclusions; for every statement is the result of a series of careful observations made of children, under all the circumstances of their daily lives.

The happiness of childhood is a sacred trust placed in our hands, and the responsibility lies with us of promoting and guarding it, unselfishly and wisely. It is something to be able to give to human beings a few short years of happiness; but this is not the end. Childhood soon passes away, and the years of labour and care are long; but then comes the time when, as Carlyle says, " the man finds that he can do without happiness, for instead thereof he finds blessedness." Now this blessedness of the life of later years, is, we believe, but the ripening of those early blossoms of happiness, that make bright the days of childhood; and it is with this most important consideration also in view that we would press so strongly on those who have the training of the next generation in their hands that they should endeavour by all means in their power to seek and to preserve the Happiness of Childhood.

"MOTHERS' SONG AND TALK."

By ELEONORE HEERWART.

THIS lecture is intended for Kinder-Garten teachers, in order to draw their attention to a book which contains Fröbel's principles, and shows his way of training little children; it is therefore a guide-book for those who have set themselves the task of spreading the knowledge of a rational and, at the same time, philosophical education. Students of Fröbel's theory, above all, must study his original works, and not be satisfied with abridgments and adaptations. The fountain-head supplies the living spring, which will impart freshness and buoyancy.

In our work, especially, we continually need to be re-invigorated, as we are surrounded by so many prejudices and obstacles, and as we hear numerous objections, which tend to damp our enthusiasm or shake our convictions.

However, for those who do not read German, there is now an American translation of the "Mutter und Kose Lieder," with a preface by Miss Peabody. Much can be learned on this subject also from the second part of "Child and Child Nature;"* and besides these, several efforts have been made to translate the songs into English, which translations, however, exist only in manuscript.

* A translation of Baroness Marenholz-Bülow's book, published by Sonnenschein und Allen.

The most familiar games out of the book, with explanations, will be found in "Music for the Kinder-Garten." (Boosey and Co.)

I purpose to speak chiefly to Kinder-Garten teachers, who would like to become acquainted with one of Fröbel's books, which is not easy to translate into English, and which is really not translatable into any language but that of a mother's sweet conversation and loving tones to her darling child.

A mother will understand the substance of this book; a mere critic or casual observer will not. *For* mothers Fröbel has written it; *from* mothers he has learnt what he has written; and therefore it might be asked, "What have others to do with it?" It was, however, to *women* that Fröbel has given his charge, when he addressed the meeting on that memorable day, June 24th, 1840, in Blankenburg (a small town in the principality of Schwarzburg Rudolstadt, Thüringen, Germany), from which place and date the Kinder-Garten may be said to have originated.

All women may act as universal mothers; in all kinds of relationships they must manifest a motherly spirit; and from this no teacher must exempt herself—least of all, a Kinder-Garten teacher.

The book, therefore, of which we speak to-night, addresses itself to all who take charge of children, and thus represent the mother. What does it mean when a mother brings you a child into the Kinder-Garten?

I understand it thus: "I bring you my child; take care of it as *I* would do;" or, "Do with my child what it is right to do;" or, "Do with it better than I am able." A silent agreement is made between the parents and you, the teacher; the child is passed from hand to hand, from heart to heart: what else *can* you do but be a mother to the little one, for the hour, morning, or day, when you have the sacred charge of a young soul? In hope and trust the child is brought to you, and you have to show yourself worthy of the confidence which is placed in your skill, your experience, or your knowledge. We thus identify the teacher with the mother, and even include every one, who is in the presence of a little child, among those who have duties to fulfil, and who might learn of Fröbel how to perform them.

This book, " Mutter und Kose Lieder," or " Mother's Song and Talk," was published in 1843.

Fröbel's first wife, who died in 1839, had furnished him with valuable materials; the family circles of his friends in Keilhau had given him opportunities of watching the development of little children (for he had none of his own); the beautiful landscapes on hill and dale, which surrounded him, had ever shown to him that children must be brought up in harmony with nature; his own loss of a mother's tender care made him the more appreciate the importance of a mother's love in early infancy; and his own experience of the social life for which children must be prepared, all are causes which resulted in the issue of this book.

In it Fröbel addresses the mother; he speaks to her in language that must surprise everyone, for he seems to feel in his own heart all the vibrations of love, joy, hope, fear, and anxiety which a mother only knows when watching her infant; but he also expects her to know her duty thoroughly. She must understand that every movement, every cry, every smile of her little one, are indications of an inward development. The child soon shows the germs of physical, mental, and moral abilities, and these must be nurtured, protected, and guided.

In this book Fröbel puts in the mother's lips *such* words, and he fancies her heart is full of *such* music, as make her seem as though she felt her dignity and responsibility. " A child" suggests the idea of a " gift from God" to Fröbel, as it did to the Hebrews of old; and to Him it must be brought again, as Hannah did with Samuel.

The mother should see a "three-fold heaven" united in the possession of her child—namely, the happiness of past, present, and future—and hers is the sacred duty of preserving that happiness.

The words Faith, Love, Hope; or Light, Love, and Life, are the types of her feelings and actions towards the child who lies before her in the cradle.

The child's smile is to the mother the sign of health, of bodily comfort, and the beginning of the joyous laughter that will ring through the house in future years, if health and happiness have been preserved. A cry will find an echo in her heart; she hastens to open her ever-ready arms, and, by her love, her wisdom and her skill, soothes the pain, and does not rest until she sees the welcome smile again.

A movement of arms or feet teaches her that the child feels its strength and wants to use it. She helps, she lifts, she teaches, and while playing with her infant's hands and feet, she is never short of a talk or song.

The Clappers in the Mill, the sound of which reach her ear, suggest the up and down movement of the feet.

"The Weathercock" (No. 9), that of the hands and wrist.

"The Clock" (No. 12), that of the arms.

"The Mowing of the Grass" (No. 13), and

"The Swimming of the Fishes" (No. 16), that of the arms and whole body.

"The Baker" (No. 18).

"The Bird's Nest" (No. 19).

"The Pigeonhouse" (No. 21).

"The Piano" (No. 26).

"The Wheelwright" (No. 45).

"The Carpenter" (No. 46), that of the hands.

Thus Fröbel provides a series of pages for the mother, which contain Pictures, Mottoes, Verses and Music.

In looking at the whole book we find that it may be divided

into four portions, each of which has its peculiar feature; namely,—
1. The Symbolical.
2. The Emotional.
3. The Practical.
4. The Explanations.

A few hints must suffice in speaking about the first and second parts.

I.—THE SYMBOLICAL.

On the outside cover of the book are the words

>Mother's Love,
>Mother's Song,
>Mother's Play.

The figures represent the mother holding her boy and girl in her arms; the former already turns his face outward as if to say, "Into the wide, wide world I'll go!" The girl clings to her mother, as if to say, "Here is my home." At the mother's feet are scattered roses and thorns, the representation of the way in which the children will repay her care in the future.

On the other side of the cover is a picture of the father, who protects his daughter and leads his son; the words round the border meaning

>Clear mind,
>Noble actions,
>Pious courage.

The title-page shows us a little picture of a mother who is surrounded by her own and neighbour's children, whom she teaches, she knowing the meaning of the call,

"Come, let us live for our Children!"

Then there are a boy and girl who are busy in a garden; another girl looks into the depths of a lily; her brother enjoys the fragrance of the flower. *He* stands on a cube, *she* on a ball. (Kinder-Garten teachers will here see a reference to the symbolical meaning of the 2nd gift).

Art and nature are interwoven on this page. Pillars, richly decorated, point heavenwards; from above shines the sun on the picture below, and the stars unite in forming a crown, which will await the mother when she enters heaven. The angel of peace is represented as descending upon the scene, and making it into an earthly paradise.

II.—THE EMOTIONAL.

The second portion contains one picture and seven pieces of poetry, which tells us what the mother would feel on beholding her infant, in whose rosy cheeks, wondering eyes, and chubby hands and feet, she delights. See page 2 of "Mutter und Kose Lieder," the song set to most appropriate music, "O Kindchen du mein."

III.—THE PRACTICAL.

The third portion is the practical or educational part. The series of pictures and songs are scenes taken from children's life in country parts of Germany, and more particularly from the part where Fröbel lived during the years 1838 to 1844; namely, in Keilhau and Blankenburg. Indoors and out of doors, in the yard, garden, field, wood, and in the workshops, the children are represented. Birds, fishes, domestic and wild animals, come before their notice; trees, flowers, wind and water, sun, moon and stars, attract their attention, and rouse their admiration. What a world of wonders! what a range for observation! What varied sources from which to gather knowledge! and what use the mother makes of all this! There is not a movement outside that she cannot imitate with the child; and thus she creates pleasant moments, and numerous physical exercises, by which she fixes the subject more firmly upon her child's mind. The fingers, hands, wrists, arms, legs or whole body, are strengthened by imitating the Weathercock Clock, the Mowing, the Baking, the Pigeons, Chickens and Hare. Even for the fingers alone, the mother knows special movements, so that a toy is always at hand—the cheapest toy in the world—one's own fingers! The mother also knows that it is necessary to train the senses, not only because books on education speak often of that training, but because she knows her child has active organs of the senses which want to do something, since the mind is longing for food, which the senses convey. The ear must hear language, music, the gentle accents and warning voices of father and mother; it must distinguish the sounds of the wind, water, the noises of animals, and when the ear has been trained to distinguish *external* sounds, it will learn to listen to the voice of conscience and of God. (See "Mutter und Kose Lieder," Picture 51, the Cuckoo). The eyesight is directed to objects far and near, the pigeons flying (Picture 15), the hares running (Picture 33), the light flickering on the wall, and farther away still are the calm beauty of the moon, and the twinkling stars in the dark blue sky. No wonder the little boy (Picture 30), wanted to climb up the ladder to the moon!—heaven and earth he would hold in the little span of his hand. No wonder the little girl by her mother's side (Picture 31) called the two bright stars she saw the first time in her young life, "Father and Mother Stars," for she knew who were to her the brightest stars on earth.

The senses of taste, touch, and smell, all, also, receive care and attention.

Another side of the child's development needs great care. This is the *moral* one; and many an opportunity the mother finds for developing it.

The pictures of "All's Gone" (No. 10), "The Boy and Girl at the Fair" (Nos. 52 and 53), are lessons on contentment.

The "Grassmowing" (No. 13), "The Target-maker" (No. 17), "The Charcoal-burners" (No. 38), "The Builder" (No. 39), and the "Wheelwright" (No. 45), teach respect for others.

"The Wolf" (No. 34), and "The Boar" (No. 35), contain warnings against greediness.

"The Fishes" (No. 16), "The Bird's Nest" (No. 19), speak against cruelty to animals.

"The Visitors and the Children" (Nos. 47, 48, 49), are about behaviour in the presence of strangers.

"The Clock" (No. 12), and "The Baker" (No. 18), are lessons on punctuality.

"The Grassmowing" (No. 13), "The Charcoal Burners" (No. 38), "The Carpenter" (No. 39), "The Brook" (No. 40), and "The Joiner" (No. 46), teach our dependence on the help of others.

The affections also need nourishment, and the manner of stimulating them is suggested in the pictures of "The Child falling, and the Mother lifting it up" (No. 8), "The Flower-basket" (No. 20), and the "Pigeon-house" (No. 21); and the religious training receives special care in "The Brook" (No. 40), and the "Church-door" (No. 54).

The artistic tastes, too, are not forgotten in this book, being specially recognized in the picture of the "Piano and Fingers" (No. 26), "Drawing" (No. 55), and the "Window" (No. 37), for architecture. Poetry also accompanies every picture.

Without force or hurry the child has learned to know the world it lives in. Unconsciously it moves through the wonders of nature, guided by the hand of father and mother; but *they* are conscious of what they have taught the child. All its powers must be unfolded, because a harmonious education is the plan they have laid out for it. They are aware of their sacred duties; they feel that an immortal soul is given to their charge. Nothing is too small for their notice that concerns its welfare—nothing too trifling; but in all its movements, silent wishes, and gentle hints, they see the "Father of the man."

So much, to night, for the practical part of the book.

IV.

The last division contains the explanations of the pictures by Fröbel himself—where he says:—

"Now, after fifty years, it is clear to me what I have longed for since I was a boy. Will it be fifty and more years before thou, oh, mother! knowest what thy child's life requires of thee?"

The child's education is thus grounded, and his affections established at home; and on this foundation the Kindergarten teacher is to build her training, which must be in perfect harmony with the former. This book, therefore, must also be *her* guide-book. As Fröbel himself says of it; that in it he has "laid down his principles; and whoever understands this book, understands also what is his aim." The finger, hand, and arm exercises furnish the Kindergarten teacher with numerous games; those which were played in the nursery can be continued in a larger circle of children. Examples thereof are the "Pigeon-house," "Fishes," "Basket," "Bird's Nest," and "Weathercock"; and adaptations, as the "Chickens," "Garden," "Clocks," "Hare," "Brook," "Cooper," and "Cuckoo."

The Kindergarten teacher recognizes the child's power of imitation, which was so easily trained, and she suggests more difficult actions that may be imitated; but she checks what is not to be copied. Certain animals have graceful movements and gentle habits, others have not.

Fröbel gives us an example of the latter in the picture of the "Wild Boar and Wolf."

That of the boar may seem strange to us here; but in some forests in Germany they are kept in large numbers—as, for instance, in the mountains and park of the Prince of Schwarzburg Rudolstadt (whence the scenes in pictures 34 and 35 were taken), several hundreds of these animals are kept.

A word has to be added about the poetry, music, and pictures themselves. Fröbel composed the verses; but he was not a poet. The rules of an artistic form were no hindrance to him when an idea had to be expressed. Many times he succeeded in his poetry, many times he did not. What does it matter? We must do it better if we can. The music and drawings were executed under his direction to express what he meant, and they may be, and have been, attacked by both artists and amateurs. Many songs are too high and too difficult, but the leading idea is in every one. The drawings have faults in their human and animal figures; but they were done by Fr. Unger, who was more of a landscape painter that a painter of figures.

Much can be said, but this sketch may help you in finding out the hidden treasures of this extraordinary book, which begins with the words:—

"Let us live for our children," and
"There is deep meaning in children's play."

Extracts from "CHILD AND CHILD-NATURE," *with reference to Fröbel's* "MUTTER U. KOSELIEDER."

The key-note of the book is the analogy between the development of humanity from its earliest infancy, and that of the individual. The fact that the germs of all human faculties and dispositions, as they show themselves in the life of humanity, in its passions, its efforts after culture, its whole manner of existence, are traceable in the nature of children as manifested in their instinctive utterances, this fact, I say, must be taken into account, in order that the games of children may be turned to their natural purpose, viz., the assistance of the child's development.

And even Fröbel in the book in question has only taken the first step towards the attainment of this purpose, has done no more than point out in what manner it is possible. The filling up of gaps in the system, greater perfection of arrangement, and improvement in the outward form will not be difficult when, through more universal practical application, Fröbel's great educational theory meets with more and more thorough understanding. Genius has but to give utterance to its thoughts, and they will in due time become embodied in appropriate forms.

Fröbel rightly calls this book a *family book*, for only by its use in the family, in the hands of mothers, can it fulfil its purpose, and contribute towards raising the family to a level of human culture corresponding to the advanced civilization of the day, and preparing mothers for their vocation in the highest sense.

Fröbel made his " Mutter u. Koselieder" the foundation of his lectures to Kindergarten teachers on his theory, and over and over again repeated : "I have here laid down the fundamental ideas of my educational theory; whoever has grasped the pivot idea of this book understands what I am aiming at. But how many do understand it? Learned men have too great a contempt for the book to give it more than cursory attention; and the majority of mothers only see in it an ordinary picture-book with little songs. No doubt there are finer pictures and better verses to be had than mine, but of what use are they if wanting in any educational power? Only a small minority of people get from my book a real understanding of my educational theory in all its fulness, but, if only mothers and teachers would follow its guidance they would at last see, in spite of all opposition, that I am right."

1. That the first mental development of the child goes on in its play, and that this play needs, consequently, to be as much systematized as the instruction imparted at a later age.

2. That by rightly meeting and assisting the natural force which vents itself in play, or by faulty and mistaken treatment of it, it may be directed either to good—*i.e.*, to its true use—or to evil—*i.e.*, its abuse ; and

3. That the examples given in the "Mutter und Koselieder" are psychologically based on the instinctive life of the child, even though they are not always expressed in the most perfect form.

However much or little the nature of children may have been studied, no one has come up to Fröbel in his searching analysis of every phase and detail of their development. Following the example of modern natural science, which has descended from the study of the greatest phenomena to that of the least, and is making its most important discoveries through microscopic investigations, Fröbel, in the field of human nature, goes back to the smallest beginnings, and finds thus the first link in the chain which connects one moment of human development with all the others. He finds the law which lies at the bottom of all systematic development, and discovers the means for the application of this law. In the growth of the child he sees the same system of law as in organic growth generally, and he points out the complete analogy between the development of the child and that of the organisms of Nature and of humanity as an organic whole.

During the first years of life the physical development is the most marked and prominent, but the growth of the soul, though unperceived, goes on, nevertheless, all the while; for in infancy body and soul are still completely in union, and can only be developed through mutual interaction. It is on this principle that Fröbel has compiled his "Mutter u. Koselieder." The games introduced in this book are adapted both to cultivating the limbs and senses, and guiding and assisting the mind in its first awakening stage.

When a child of about a year old is taken out of doors, the things that first attract its notice are those that move. Movement signifies to children *life*, and is what they first become aware of. Hence the child's glance will at once be arrested by a weather-cock, or any other object, moved by the wind.

The child awakens to life in its mother's arms, its mother is, so to say, its own wider life. Without her care, without her looks of love, existence would offer a sorry prospect to the young new-comer. The mother must be her child's first mediator with the world and mankind.

'The first utterance through which the child expresses its love-relationship to human beings, to its mother, is *smiling*. The human heart alone is capable of laughter and tears, and for the newborn infant this is the only language at command to express its wants and feelings.

Extracts from "Music for the Kindergarten," *by Eleonore Heerwart.*

We head the list of these games with four from Fröbel's "Mutter und Koselieder," which may also be played only as a finger and arm exercise;" but these four—"The Basket," "The Weathercock," "The Pigeon-house," and "The Bird's-nest," do not exclude others from being used as proper finger-games, for we might also act "Gentle Bee," "The Fishes," "The Clappers," "The Trees," "The Sawyer," "The Clocks," "The Cooper;" nor does it mean that the first four games are *only* finger and arm exercises; on the contrary, they are used in the Kindergarten as real Kindergarten games, especially "The Pigeon-house;" but we wish to point out that most of the games can be played at home, with one, two, or more children, as well as with a larger number in the Kindergarten, and they will then furnish mothers with suitable conversations and pleasant employments when they spend their time in the sweet companionship of their little ones.

In fact, Fröbel meant "The Basket," "The Pigeon-house," &c., for the use of home, and wrote them especially for mothers. Their adaptation to the Kindergarten was a secondary thought.

A Kindergarten game means a game which is played by many children, and conducted by a "teacher." The subject is chosen from daily life, from nature, and especially from the sphere in which the child lives.

The object of the game is to spend a happy hour with the children, to teach them the words, music, and time, and make these bear upon the child's physical, mental, and moral development.

"THE BASKET."—No. 48.

This arm-and-hand exercise is translated from Fröbel's "Mutter und Koselieder, No. 20," the picture of which shows us children who are gathering flowers, supposed to have been planted by themselves. The flowers are to be given to the father as a birthday present. The mutual affection between parents and children will grow when it is nourished, and will remain the strongest tie on earth.

As a game in the Kindergarten, it may be played by holding little baskets filled with flowers, or by holding the hands in the shape of baskets, the thumbs representing the handle. A graceful movement of the body, and swinging up and down of the arms, keeping time with the music, will give life to the game.

"THE WEATHERCOCK."—No. 49.

If asked, "What is the first plaything for children?" we may reply, "Their own hands," for these are always near, and cost no money.

Always to find something for the active little fingers to do, is a great task to many mothers; but let Fröbel teach them from his book of "Mutter und Koselieder" how many things the little fingers can imitate, and they will no longer be at a loss for a game.

The child, in looking at the tops of houses, may happen to see a weathercock being turned by the wind. Immediately the mother seizes the opportunity for telling the child to imitate it with its arms and hands. The arm from the elbow must be held erect, and the hand at right angles with it, turned with the inside towards the face. When the song begins the hand is turned outwards, and for every bar one movement is made. The wrist especially is strengthened by this exercise.

"THE PIGEON-HOUSE."—No. 50.

Is it necessary to suggest how "The Pigeon-house" should be played? It should be remembered that the children always form a ring, which in this case should be a closed one, to enable the children to say, "My pigeon-house I open wide." A step or two backwards will widen the ring; the arms a little raised will allow the pigeons to fly out and about, until the words "But soon they return" be heard, when they fly in again to sing their soft "Coo, coo."

The pigeons may tell where they have been, and what they have seen in the fields.

Other pigeons are then chosen, who do the same.

To vary the game, there may be a farmer who owns the pigeons, and who fixes the hour when the house should be opened. The sound of a clock striking the hour may be imitated.

If Fröbel had left us no other game than this one, it alone would entitle him to be called "the children's friend," for it has given joy to many little ones.

"THE BIRD'S-NEST."—No. 51.

Children are delighted when they see birds, but they must learn to see and spare them.

In his book of "Mutter und Koselieder" Fröbel gives us a picture, a verse, and a lesson, that we may know how to cultivate in children love for birds, and respect for the parental feelings of the feathered tribe. There would be no throwing of stones at swallows' nests under the eaves of houses, nor climbing of trees to take the eggs away, and other cruelties, if in every house and every place where children meet the life of birds were made the subject of talk, song, and a simple finger or hand game such as " The Bird's-nest."

It may form the introduction to the following game, or succeed a story and description of birds.

The children may either sit or stand when they play " The Bird's-nest."

The hands imitate the shape of the nest. The thumbs represent the old birds.

It is well to mention the name of a special bird, as linnet, robin, &c.

"THE FISHES."—No. 62.

According to Fröbel's "Mother's Song and Talk," Picture No. 16, the little child, after having become acquainted with the familiar world at home, is now introduced into a new scene, where, in the cool forest, a silvery brook winds its way over rocks, between grasses, and rushes, and shady trees.

New life shows itself before the wondering eyes of the child; it hears the rustling of the branches, the singing of the birds, the splashing of the hasty brook, and it sees the golden lights between the tall trees, the soft green moss; and in the clear water the astonished child discovers the trout, for the first time in his life. The little boy thinks, "That little fish is quick, but I will be quicker," and into the water he makes his way. After some fruitless attempts he succeeds in catching a little trout, which he hands to his sister, who stands on the bank and watches the movements of her brother. She holds the little fish and looks at the large eyes, the glittering scales, the forked tail, which moves to and fro : but all at once it stops !—the eyes !—the trout is dead ! For the first time in her young life she sees a creature dead in her hand, by *her* hand, or at any rate by her brother's hand. She calls him,

H

shows the dead fish, and the boy's yet unhardened heart also feels that he has caused the death of the little trout. He had only wished to play, and did not mean harm. For his whole life he may have learned a lesson that even in play we must count the cost in order to make it what it should be, a harmless game at the least. There in the solitude of the wood, by the silvery brook, the early cruelty was checked by the first sad experience. A boy not yet spoilt by harsh, inconsistent, superficial treatment, righted himself by the dictates of his sorrowing heart.

The game of the fishes, which is derived from this picture, teaches us to imitate their movements, but not to persecute the fishes. Although the remark seems superfluous it may be permitted here, for it gives the rule for all games in the Kindergarten and for all children, that cruelty should in no way be represented.

The ring is the pond, some children are fishes and imitate swimming by a movement of their arms, and the diving and rising by stooping when the song indicates it. The movement should be practised by all the children, as it requires great attention, owing to the $3/8$-time in each bar. The subjects for conversation are very many before and after the game, and may be varied according to the kind of fish which is chosen. In no other game is it more necessary for the Kindergarten teacher to be acquainted with the habits and structures of the animals, as in this all vague and undecided answers of the children should be rejected.

WASTED FORCES.

By EMILY SHIRREFF.

—◆—

It is a subject of melancholy contemplation to the friends of education, that after public recognition of its importance for so many years, in some parts of the continent of Europe for a period of more than half a century, no great material results of its influence have yet become manifest. Nations that were careless and pleasure-loving before, show the same spirit still; the unthrifty have not mended their ways; the worshippers of gold have not set up nobler idols; the military spirit has not decreased; the indolent indifferentism that takes no interest in public affairs till roused by some great crisis, still reigns where it reigned before; those who believed that new eras may be inaugurated by the stroke of a pen or the machinations of secret societies, still hold their belief. In short, the great masses of mankind through the most civilized nations of the world show little trace of the efforts made to raise, through education, their moral and intellectual condition.

We are an educational society, and this question is one which must interest us deeply; for either we are wrong in attributing so much influence to education, or we ought to be able to discern the causes that have so far neutralised that influence. The inquiry is, however, so large that we must limit ourselves to a small portion of it. We must leave aside the consideration of the wide social and political causes that are antagonistic to the spread of the sounder views and principles which should be the result of wide-spread education, and confine ourselves to strictly educational considerations. Among these, three points deserve special attention :—1st, That while calling it education, we have actually given only elementary instruction. 2ndly, That the earliest and most plastic period of life has been neglected, thus leaving an almost impossible task to be performed in the succeeding one. 3rdly, That the educational power of women has been neglected, left, to an enormous extent, untrained and unused.

These three points are closely connected, the one with the other, and are all intimately bound up with our own work as a Froebel Society. The first will scarcely be contested by any one. The utmost endeavours of elementary schools barely compass giving the first and simplest notions of necessary knowledge, with more or less use of the instruments for acquiring more, and such general benefit as results from the order and discipline of school life, and the influence of moral and religious teaching, whose precepts are too often at variance with the whole experience of the children out of school. If this were really education, we could only laugh at our own folly in expecting such large results from so small a thing. When we speak of benefiting a people by education, we must mean that the mass of men and women should learn how to think more clearly, to judge more correctly, to act according to more fixed principles, to have, in short, more common sense and juster notions of duty; and finally, to have perception enough of the difference between ignorance and knowledge to wish to take advantage of such opportunities as life may present to them to add to their stock of acquirements.

How far the education of the well-to-do classes of any nation has hitherto produced such results generally, I will not inquire into here; but what right have we to expect they shall follow from the reading and writing and other small achievements of the elementary school? Yet, I believe such achievements to be as much as schools can compass at present. Better methods might, doubtless, produce some improvement; and just views of education would do yet more; but time fails for what has to be accomplished; the imperative necessities of life limit the years that can be given to school instruction, and the work of those years is rendered doubly heavy by the neglect of those that have gone before.

The infant-school system is designed to remedy some of these defects, and there is no doubt of the great benefits it has conferred. Unfortunately, the very large numbers taught together in these schools render nugatory much of the endeavours to educate them. They are of an age to require individual attention, and they are dealt with in masses. The general influence on character of the order, regularity, obedience, cleanliness enforced, is inestimable; but with regard to strictly intellectual development, the system was not originally constructed on a scientific plan, and the effects are rather incidental than direct fruits of this method. The object-lessons are good, but they do not promote the natural development of faculty like the Kinder-Garten exercises, and the manipulations of the latter are altogether wanting. The direct teaching is intended to prepare for later school-work, but it prepares by laying a foundation of reading and writing; not the foundation of quickened faculties, exercised heads, and habits of comparing and judging, of speaking and moving accurately, which is the preparation of the Kinder-Garten. In short, these schools, invaluable as they have been, do an imperfect work, and of the vast numbers who have never been brought even under their influence, it is not too much to say that the child comes under the schoolmaster's hands, not ignorant merely, but with his moral and intellectual growth already warped. Rapid expansion of faculty has been going on from his birth, unwatched and undirected, and most of what he has learnt for himself has been inaccurately learnt, or rather hinders than aids the instruction he now comes to receive. Thus the second point indicated above, the neglect of the early period of life during which the mental and physical growths are so important, is evidently a principal cause of the failure of education, and it is a cause with which we, as the Froebel Society, are immediately concerned. If education is not only to give instruction, but to discipline the faculties and bring them into fit condition for observing, learning, and thinking aright, it is obvious that the whole of this work cannot begin at once. The child must have gradually learnt to use his mental powers as he has learnt to use his limbs and bodily strength before we exact from him any systematic exertion of the one or the other. While he is still quite incapable of acquiring abstract or general knowledge, he is capable of learning to observe correctly what is before him, and to draw a right inference from one thing he really understands to another, which is the foundation of all accurate study and thought hereafter. The child inevitably uses his faculties as he uses his limbs. The only question is, whether he shall grope with the former, or learn to use them rightly and with a purpose, as he learns to walk or to throw a ball. This is an obvious and quite elementary truth to any disciples of Froebel, and the Kinder-Garten is designed to supply this early education, or such portion of it as can be given out of home; but to the ordinary framers of educational systems, national or other, it has not yet been made obvious, and so they neglect little children and hope that book learning will at a later period do the work of education.

The third point I have mentioned is inevitably bound up with this question of infant training; for that early portion of child life is altogether in the hands of women, either as mothers, nurses, or teachers, and if their educational power has been neglected we can hope for no reform that will lay a better foundation for the after-work of the schoolmaster, or afford him that help he requires from the co-operation of home influence. We may fearlessly lay down the axiom that education in its true sense, as a real civilizing power, will remain in abeyance till women are recognized as the natural educators, and till then we shall continue to make vain efforts to supplement with instruction the absence of the wider influence of education.

No one realized this truth more fully than Froebel, and after fruitless attempts to inaugurate a complete system of education during the ordinary school period, combining the development of faculty in children neglected up to the age of seven or eight, with the indispensable course of school instruction, he realized that education must begin from the earliest dawn of life, and that mothers must be the educators. This principle underlies his whole system; the Kinder-Garten presupposes it, and appeals to it throughout. When we give a little attention to the subject, this fact is so self-evident that we only wonder how any one could for a moment have doubted it, or mistaken the true position of women as regards education. In one sense it never has been mistaken, for that mothers must bring up their children, to use the common expression, and that when the mother's care fails, such "bringing up" must be delegated to another woman, is the most universally acknowledged fact of every-day life; but what is not so universally understood is, that the bringing-up is another name for education, and that education, to be effectual, must be conducted with a purpose and according to knowledge. Froebel did not discover a new fact, or even propound a new theory when he hailed women as the true ministers of the great work of reformation which he undertook. He only strove to give a new direction to the old activity, and to make manifest the true ground on which it should proceed. Pestalozzi, and even Rousseau before him, had made a public appeal to women; but Froebel renewed it with fresh force, and his views of education afford the simplest and fullest exposition of the duties incumbent upon them. Rightly or wrongly, for good or for ill, mothers have always and must always educate their children. Owing, doubtless, to its transcendant importance, this one great human duty, which God has placed under the safeguard of the strongest affection of woman's nature, is never consciously, wilfully neglected save by the most depraved in any class; only they call it "bringing up," not education, leaving the latter for school-years and school-discipline. This mistake is the root of endless evil. It seems an error in words only; but words are powerful things, for they help to form associations, and lead to wrong action when the associations they have formed are wrong. Froebel admitted no such distinctions between the influence of parents or teachers at one period and another, and when he speaks of education, he means one and the same continuous process, beginning in infancy, and carried on through varied phases and by various means, till the grown-up man and woman take into their own hands the task, which will end only with the close of earthly existence.

With such a view of education, when Froebel called upon women, he called upon them only to undertake their natural task, that which love and necessity equally bound upon them, with a wider and more distinct purpose; as something not apart from the later task of the schoolmaster, but preparing the way for it, laying down the preliminary lines of his work, and, indeed, overlapping it in many directions, as home-life overlaps school-life. This substitution of a definite, far-searching purpose for the instinctive mother's care, of conscious education for desultory "bringing-up," is what has never yet been accomplished, except among a small minority; and the reason is that education is ill-understood and women have not realized that if they are to undertake a serious task, the success of which depends on knowledge of its conditions, they must acquire the knowledge.

It is this duty of women to fit themselves for their natural vocation as educators that I wish to press upon your attention to-night. I need scarcely remind you how specially it bears upon our own peculiar work, which more than any other is helped by the action of mothers. There is no doubt such a thing as an instinctive gift for education, as there is for every other art which the majority of men have to acquire patiently and laboriously; and thus some women who have never studied the subject succeed in educating their children, and by their very success nourish the popular prejudice, that no special study is required for the performance of this natural duty. But when an unusually able woman, or the mother of unusually gifted children, morally or intellectually, produces an admirable result, without study of rules or principles, the way to test her success as a guide for the multitude, is to try and imagine what would be the result of the same high-handed ignorance of principles *without* the natural gifts. A system for common use must be fit for the mass of mankind, and the mass is not gifted. Every theory may safely assume the mother's love, because this is natural—all but unfailing; but it cannot assume the possession by the mother of the native power which can supply the lack of knowledge, whether of human nature, in which the principles of education have their root, or of those branches of instruction which furnish the subject-matter of education. Thence it is evident that when women are appealed to as natural educators, it is implied that they will make education their study, and acquire the knowledge requisite for assisting the mental and physical development of their children during those years which prepare the course of all future years. It is not indispensable for mothers to be teachers, but if they do not know what constitutes good teaching they will not know what results to look for. There is no need that they should have made a deep study of either physiology or mental philosophy, but unless they clearly realize that mental and bodily health depend upon conditions which can be learnt only through some elementary knowledge of those two sciences, how can they ensure those conditions for their children, or how judge if they are or are not observed in the educational institutions, Kinder-Gartens or schools in which their children are to be placed?

All school education requires the foundation, the support and complement of home education; but to the Kinder-Garten, dealing with children at such a tender age, it is absolutely indispensable, and the want of it constantly cripples the teacher's best endeavours. A child of ten years old and upwards may begin to distinguish between the teaching and general influence of school and home. He can recognize where he is most stimulated to do well, to behave well; what praise he most cares to work for; and, unfortunate as it is when the home holds a lower position in his estimate than the school, the higher influence is not lost. The little child, on the other hand, can distinguish nothing; but he suffers from the jar produced by differences of treatment he cannot understand. The work of the Kinder-Garten teacher is not indeed lost, but it is thwarted by the child being placed at home under intellectual and moral direction proceeding on different principles, or most likely no principles at all, but simply the spontaneous unreasoning action of ignorant affection. Of the many sadder cases where even such care as this does not exist, but only neglect caused by the different forms of vice or folly belonging to the different classes of society, it is needless to speak. School-training in one way or another, according to age, is then the only resource; but once more, however, good it may be, it can but partly compensate for the absence of home education, and thus the study of education by women, their serious preparation for this great duty, is the pivot on which all ultimately turns. Vain will be any hope of lifting education out of the groove of routine teaching, till this is acknowledged; till society remembers and enforces this truth: that whatever the position, occupations or other family duties of a woman, one sacred office is laid upon her who undertakes the responsibility of motherhood, and that is the care of her children in every sense in which care is needed; guarding them from suffering; promoting their bodily and spiritual welfare, aiding nature's gradual work of development in every direction. Such care is in a measure that of the physician as regards the right conditions of health, and it is also the true cure of souls. All this will be generally conceded and even looked upon as a truism; yet, I repeat, it is practically denied every day and every hour, by the assumption that such a task can be executed without study or preparation; by the assertion, implied if not put into words, that natural instincts and parental love will give the required ability for discharging the responsibilities of a parent.

We have now considered the three causes of failure I pointed out in the beginning, to explain the disappointment which has followed the high hopes of those who looked to national education as the regenerator of nations, and we have found wasted forces in three directions; 1st, The waste of labour and money in giving instruction which was vainly expected to produce the fruits of education. 2nd, Waste of that immense natural form of development of the child's faculties during the years we put to no account. 3rd, Waste of women's educational power and position, which we find fatally to involve the other two. This last, therefore, is the one which claims, on every account, our most earnest consideration, in order that, having found the central source of failure, we may, if possible, help towards finding a remedy.

So wide-spread and deep-rooted an evil is not, however, easy to reach. It is only from a higher and purer view of women's position generally, that we can hope for any wide recognition of this terrible waste of civilizing power, or any large endeavours to redeem the past. But in all practical questions reforms may begin in a corner which shall presently spread over a wide field, and, therefore, all who can persuade a few women will help to turn public opinion. It is in this belief that I have brought forward the subject this evening, thinking it well that we, who are practically concerned in education, should consult together what we can do, individually or as a society, to quicken in women, and in young mothers especially, the perception of their duty in this particular. It is our special object to win over mothers of little children to study Froebel's doctrine, and to take an interest in his method. It must then be our endeavour to present these to them in a manner which shall arrest attention and excite interest. As a society we might possibly organize some plan for spreading knowledge of the first principles of education. For real students there are plenty of good books, and now that the whole subject is taken up in a new spirit, there are excellent lectures which, we trust, are not attended by professional students only. Our work should be a preliminary one, to endeavour to inspire those who know nothing with the desire to learn something; to persuade women who have no professional inducement to take up the subject, that it is the real and sacred profession of all women who have taken upon themselves the responsibilities of motherhood. We do not want lectures on the Art of Teaching,—that may come afterwards,—but on the Art of Training, on the elementary notions of education, based on observation of the child's nature as it puts out its earliest shoots, and on the simplest methods of aiding their growth, and preserving them from any adverse influence which might thwart their development. Such teaching as might be given on a few texts from Froebel's "Song-book for Mothers," or Mdme. von Marienholtz's

"Child Nature," would give a new turn to the thoughts of many earnest, intelligent women, who have not hitherto had their attention directed to such views; and if the lectures could be illustrated practically through Kinder-Garten occupations conducted before the audience and duly explained, and could their educational value be further exemplified by reference to Mdme. de Portugall's Synoptical Table, I think we might win many converts. Probably we should win, before long, a sufficient number to form here and there new centres of information, independently of our direct action.

One of the reasons of the difficulty we find in getting Kinder-Garten training properly appreciated is, that its office in education is precisely that which has no immediately visible results, and is based on considerations strange to those who have not studied the subject. If it taught reading and writing more rapidly than other systems, that would be a tangible merit, and, for the same reason, the manual dexterity cultivated by it, is seen to be a good thing. But the cultivation of the faculties themselves, to make them more fit for future work, of developing the child's own powers in every direction instead of teaching it grammar or history—this fundamental mental discipline is only understood by those who have learnt something of what the various mental faculties are, and why such and such a mode of bringing them into action produces good or evil results. To persons who have given no attention to these things *seeing* is much the same as *observing;* little difference is perceived between knowing a thing by rote or knowing it with understanding; and reasoning suggests something for the use of the learned only, and they find it hard to believe that the same process is needed to avoid blunders in those common judgments which seem so easy. It is when we begin to disentangle these things, and thus to perceive how much has to be done to prepare the child to see, to think, to act, and to learn with some correctness, that we feel the merits of Froebel's system; and it is just this part of the study of education that we should endeavour to place before young mothers in as clear and simple a form as possible. We have, I believe, peculiar opportunities of doing so, through the medium of the Kinder-Garten itself, with its practical illustrations, and, I trust, we may seriously consider how best to enter upon this hitherto neglected phase of our work as a Froebel Society.

But apart from this action of the Society, individual teachers might help materially, if they could persuade the mothers of their pupils to enter into the subject with them; to visit the classes frequently and to read any short explanations of what they see there. We cannot doubt that the mistresses of Kinder-Gartens, having the cause at heart, would welcome the opportunities for such conversations, and they might, perhaps, do something more to create the opportunities. It might be possible to gather a few ladies together to discuss difficulties. Small meetings might be organized by competent teachers, which a few might be invited to attend, and allowed, perhaps, to bring a friend, and at these, the occupations could be practically exhibited more fully than with a class of children, and their inter-dependence and educational value explained. Great good might, I feel convinced, be done in this way. Here a few and there a few would be won to intelligent comprehension of the system, and their example and advocacy would win others. When once a little knowledge is gained, the more earnest minds will not stop there; when interest is really kindled, the inspiring spirit will be kindled too.

Members of the society who are not teachers might, at least, lead those who want knowledge to the sources where it may be found; they can speak their own convictions, though they may have no practical familiarity with the method; they may persuade any of their own friends who are inclined to send their children to the Kinder-Garten, to become scholars themselves. All minor difficulties will vanish if mothers learn enough to feel the value of what their children are learning. The Kinder-Garten would assume quite a new importance in their eyes, and there would be many earnest endeavours to bring the home management into harmony with it.

And now I can hear objectors say: "Supposing you have done your utmost with the women of the educated classes, how does this view of mothers' duty apply to the far more numerous class of the uneducated? If it is as educators of the race that we appeal to women, the appeal must include them also." Perfectly true; but it can reach them only through the medium of their happier sisters, and the general influence of higher views. It is only too certain that education, like all other benefits of human knowledge, will ever be relative to the class addressed. Means and leisure must ultimately give the measure of what can be attained, however just and liberal the system under which we live. But what we may expect is that more and more as true Christian civilization grows among us, those who have most intellectual advantages will facilitate to those who have least, the acquirement of what tends to elevate their condition as human beings. If it is reckoned even now a fair measure of justice to put all grades of instruction within reach of the poor man who aspires to culture, still more must it be simple justice to bring to every home that degree of instruction which is needed for the better fulfilment of a great duty. Hence I cannot doubt that as society awakens to the importance of the universal educating power of mothers, means will be found to spread universally that simple knowledge of first principles, which will rescue infancy from a very large portion, at least, of the ignorant treatment that now stunts, when it does not distort, the normal growth of mind and body. We see various subjects taken up for adult instruction among women, not one of which approaches in importance this one, or is so likely to kindle interest and rouse native power in the hearers. We have cooking classes and sanitary lectures and mothers' meetings, &c. Why should not the education of little children be the subject of instruction given in the same manner—given widely, frequently and earnestly, by women who have themselves had every opportunity of acquiring the knowledge they would impart. And let us remember that such instruction will be greatly helped by the appeal it makes to the strongest feelings of the woman's heart, however rough or uncultivated she may be. When a few real disciples are won from among the many, they will in their turn become apostles. Each reformed home will become a centre of good example, until gradually, however slowly, a new sense of duty is created; and public opinion, become more enlightened, will find the means of continuing with greater facilities, the work set on foot by the zeal of a few.

Since the foregoing pages were written, a great controversy has been going on concerning the pressure put upon children by modern school-teaching, in which, doubtless, many present have taken a keen interest. It would be out of place here to enter into the details of that controversy; I only wish to point out, how largely it all ultimately turns upon the serious deficiency I have dwelt upon this evening—upon the ignorance of mothers with regard to education. If mothers were penetrated with the truth that they *must* educate their children themselves, whoever else may assist them, whether in giving instruction or in any other way, these disputes would not arise or would be quickly settled. Children would go to school with due mental preparation. If sent to a day-school they would remain under the same watchful maternal care for the far larger portion of their lives still spent at home. The twenty hours a week, or thereabouts, spent under the school tuition, would not be supposed to exonerate from responsibility the parents who control the remaining 148 hours; but the responsibility would be discharged with knowledge of what it involves, and knowledge of each individual child, and the mother would be capable of consulting intelligently with the school-teacher, and of laying down a scheme of home life and study which should co-operate with, instead of thwarting the school scheme. Naturally, mistakes would still occur on both sides, but we should never see the misconception, the antagonism, the divided, often contrary influence, the early neglect and the impatient ambitions that thwart the work of the best schools now. The least we should expect of mothers who had some knowledge, however slight, of education, would be that if, for any reason, they wish to be rid of the charge of their children, they should send them to boarding, and not to day-schools, since the chief advantage and merit of the latter is that they still leave the greater part of the child's life under parental management and influence.

I would not, however, close these remarks without saying a few words in extenuation of what may appear to some very severe and undeserved strictures upon mothers generally, whose earnest desire to do their duty I never doubt, even when, in my opinion, they fall most sadly short of it. There is nothing strange in the fact that women have neglected to study education, or at least to study it on scientific grounds, and nothing for which, in the past, they could be held seriously to blame. Their neglect was that of the nation at large. Education has never, till of late years, held its rightful place in this country. The subject has been simply a practical one, to be solved by putting children under tuition for a certain number of years, in order that they might acquire such knowledge as might be wanted for use, or show, according to the station in life they were to occupy. Moral training was always, thank God, more seriously thought of; but rather as a part of religion than of education. Women themselves were denied all serious culture, and the very fact that the training of young children is necessarily women's work, was sufficient to class it as trivial work. Women being unused to study and reflection, naturally

I

acquiesced in the opinions prevailing around—and this state of things must be very slow to change among the majority, immense as the improvement has been among the few. It is a slow and painful process, as we too well know, for an individual to repent and amend; it is yet more difficult and laborious for a nation; what then must it be when half the human race, fettered in its development by the errors of the other half and its own, awakes from its mental torpor to recognize the neglected duties, the slighted responsibilities, which have been so many snares to themselves, and so many occasions of evil and mischief to others? Very slowly can those who have inherited this burden come to the full consciousness of what it is now incumbent upon them to do; and very slowly will the great number grope their way towards doing it. It is well to remember this when we seem to blame *persons*, and are rather blaming the *conditions* under which they have grown up and lived.

It would be impossible to estimate what society has suffered from neglecting, nay, stifling the educating powers of women; and if ever real civilization is to be attained, if ever we are to see more than a nominal Christianity triumph, if the moral force of humanity is ever to be drawn out fully and harmoniously with the intellectual force and spirit to predominate over matter, it must be, in large measure, by the rightful influence of women, created mostly through education, and thus permeating society through all the channels of private life, creating associations, forming habits, moulding social opinion. Such is the power which nature placed women in a position to exercise through their sway over men's best affections, their social influence, the greater moral purity and refinement which tends to keep the higher spiritual interests predominant over the lower material, the imaginative over the calculating, the unselfish over the narrow utilitarian; and lastly, and once again, through their unlimited power over early childhood, by which they can instil and perpetuate the best habits and associations of their own lives. Such, I repeat, is the sway which nature gave women to exercise, and of which, through ignorance, through the faults born of a depressed condition, they have been careless, while too often seeking compensation for their outward dependence by the easy sway over men's passions and vanity.

But now, we trust, the time is come when they will rouse themselves to nobler aims. The cry for education sounds through every nation, and Government after Government takes it up, and laws are passed, and schools built and teachers appointed; yet, as I said before, even in those countries where this has gone on longest, we find but small results on the character of the people. And why? because instruction has been common and education very rare; because women, with whom the strongest educating power rests, have been inert. Now, let women once be fired with the noble ambition of fulfilling in its highest sense the mission Heaven has laid upon them, and the dawn of a better era may, at length, be seen.

THE KINDER-GARTEN

IN RELATION TO SCHOOLS.

By Emily Shirreff.

It has seemed to me that on the occasion of this third annual meeting of our Society, I could not choose a more important question to dwell upon than that of the relation of the Kinder-Garten to schools,—in other words, of this peculiar form of infant training to the system of instruction which will fashion the next periods of childhood and early youth. How will the one affect, or be affected, by the other? This is the question on which the wide acceptance of Froebel's method must ultimately hang. Could it be shown that after education will be hindered or in any way rendered more difficult by it, clearly all efforts to introduce it must stop. Could it be supposed to be a matter of indifference—neither to make, nor mar, the after-work of school—then it would remain a matter of mere choice or fancy for individual parents to decide as they like; but if it can be shown that all the work of the Kinder-Garten is laying a more solid foundation, or tracing more direct paths for the workers of a later period, then it behoves us to give a hearty national welcome to this foreign system, and to work it with zealous good will. And this is the conviction with which I speak to you to-night, the conviction on which our society is founded. As we hope that there are many strangers among us this evening, it would be very desirable to give some slight sketch of Froebel's system; but in a paper such as this, without the means of demonstration and with much other matter pressing, it is scarcely possible, and I can only touch briefly on the chief characteristics of his method.

Froebel is perhaps over-rated by a few, but he is sadly under-rated by the great majority even of those who make education their business;—if they made it their *study* it might be otherwise. This misconception of Froebel's work comes partly from ignorance of his life, of the history of his labour to establish the principles he adopted in his youth, and to which in his old age he gave partial expression in the Kinder-Garten. It was the whole scope of education, the whole training of man to do his duty in a loving spirit to God and man, that occupied all the best years of his life. The title of his book, "The Education of Mankind," itself shows how wide was its purpose. But men were too eager for knowledge to attend to the culture of the human being; and everywhere instruction overlaid education. Thus the conviction was forced upon him that the real groundwork must be laid before school instruction begins. All thoughtful writers on education had felt this to a certain degree. We find the principles laid down with more or less distinctness in writings of different epochs, and Pestalozzi made it the foundation of his system. He appealed to mothers as Froebel did after him to women generally; but his system was imperfect. Froebel was the first to bring a wide study of human nature to bear upon infant life, and to reduce to system the observations thus made. His leading principle is that with a view to full harmonious development the child must be allowed to grow freely according to the laws of his nature—physical, moral, and intellectual. Growth in one direction must not be allowed to hinder or supersede growth in another. All the faculties are necessary for perfect life, and Froebel watched children closely to ascertain the order of development indicated by instinctive tendencies.

The intellectual faculties are first awakened by the child's surroundings; light and bright objects attract it even in the cradle; when it can run it manifests ceaseless curiosity about all it can see or touch, and expresses that curiosity as soon as it can speak,—the pleasure children take in all this is evident to every one, but it requires an observer to note how mental activity forms an element in that pleasure. We are accustomed to give that name only to the conscious labour of riper years, and we often overlook the fact that the very same faculties that must do the work of those years are beginning to unfold ere the child can freely speak or run about. Froebel knew that it was so, and felt that from that time also began the possibility of giving a right or a wrong bent to those faculties, of aiding or thwarting their action. "The purpose of education," says Mme. Marenholtz von Bulow, "is to aid natural development in all its fulness. Since, then, development begins with the first breath, so also does education begin then." How this may be done has been minutely laid down by Froebel in his advice to mothers, and the Kinder-Garten is the practical exposition of his principles as regards children from three to seven years of age. I can only allude to a few points. For instance, a child will exercise his observation upon everything around him, but we can place within his reach the object we wish him to observe. He will after a time reason after his own fashion; it is ours to lead him to find the right conclusions. He will be ceaselessly curious, and his curiosity is too often repressed or foolishly answered; Froebel knew that such curiosity is the root of love of knowledge, and on it he builds to make instruction a delight.

The moral side of the child's nature awakens later than the physical and intellectual, and its growth is too often blunted by over-indulgence, or by rewards and punishments; Froebel felt that it will expand only in an atmosphere of love, and the two great instruments of all education, habit and association, must be used even from the cradle to prepare the way for the exercise of will and conscience at a later day.

Physical activity, which first manifests itself in the pleasure the infant takes in moving its limbs, becomes *play* with the growing child, and as physical exercise play is generally much and rightly valued; but the mental activity drawn out in play, and forming a great part of true delight, is too commonly overlooked. Froebel recognized and saw character, imagination—the first dawning of the creative faculty—manifested in play. Having thus observed all the child's natural tendencies, he devised a system by means of which they should be healthily developed—and the system is Kinder-Garten training.

The principles, then, on which Froebel built his system may be summed up briefly under four heads:—1st.—All the faculties of the child, mental and bodily, are to be severally drawn out and exercised as far as age allows. 2nd.—The powers of habit and association—which are the great instruments of all education—of the whole training of life must be brought to bear from the earliest dawn of intelligence, with a systematic purpose. 3rd.—The active instincts of childhood are to be cultivated through manual, no less than through mental work, and such manual exercise made an essential part of the training. 4th.—The senses are to be trained to accuracy as well as the hand. The children must learn how to observe what is placed before them, and to *see it truly*, an acquirement which any teacher of science or of drawing will appreciate. To work out these principles Froebel devised his practical method of infant education, and the very name he gave to the place where his play lessons were to be given marks his purpose. We have adopted that foreign name; let us, then, see what it means.

A Kinder-Garten—not a child's garden in ordinary sense,

although such gardens form an important adjunct, but *a garden of children*—as we might say a garden of roses—a place of culture for that most wonderful thing that lives and grows upon our earth, the infant human being, and we feel at once how appropriate is that name, when we remember Froebel's views of education. We find the same kind of analogy of thought, though in the inverse order, in our term of a "nursery garden," a piece of ground where young plants are tended, as are children in the nursery, while the Kinder-Garten is the spot where children can expand and grow and enjoy life, as plants do in a garden. In the school children are taught, they are recipients of knowledge; Froebel considers them simply as being endowed with faculties of many kinds that must develop freely according to their nature, that must not be urged in this direction, or cramped in another, but be placed in the most favourable circumstances to attain their full growth according to the laws impressed on them by the Creator, as do the plants in the soil and climate that suits them.

No books are to be seen in a Kinder-Garten, because no ideas or facts are presented to the child that he cannot clearly understand and verify. The object is not to teach him arithmetic or geometry, though he learns enough of both to be very useful hereafter, but to lead him to discover facts and truths concerning numbers and lines and angles for himself. Thus in the play lessons with little wooden cubes and other figures, the teacher simply rules the order in which he shall approach a new thing, and gives him the correct names, which henceforth he must always use; but the observation of resemblances and differences (that groundwork of all knowledge), the reasoning from one point to another, and the conclusion he arrives at are all his own—he is only made to see his mistake if he makes one. Ordinary object lessons, such as Pestalozzi gave, and such as our infant schools give them, appeal to vision only to help the understanding; in the Kinder-Garten the child handles every object from which he is taught, and must learn to reproduce it. If a thing is drawn for him, or built for him, with his little bricks, he forthwith builds or draws the same for himself; his hand no less than his eye is exercised in many ways to delicate and accurate work, and the instinct of activity is thus satisfied. This simultaneous training of the senses and hands together with the mental faculties, is one striking characteristic of Froebel's system; and throughout the long series of occupations, drawing, paper-folding, plaiting, etc., this is systematically exercised. What can be thus obtained of accuracy and deftness of handling, may best be seen in the modelling which little creatures of five years old produce. Another characteristic of Froebel's system is the value for play and its adaptation to purposes of education. Through it the child's natural activity is brought into full healthy exercise, while it is so directed that the games accompanied by singing stir the imagination and cultivate all the moral qualities which we value so highly later on the school playground, habits of acting together, of bearing and forbearing, of good-humour under failure, etc.; and the words of the song keep up the interest in human actions, and in forms and changes of nature that the child has witnessed. A *third* and yet more important characteristic is the observation and love of nature. Before coming to books a child's curiosity must be satisfied about outer objects, and thus gradually transformed into intelligent interest and desire for knowledge. Not till this part of education is brought into a certain state of forwardness did Froebel consider that children should be allowed to read and write and thus approach the ordinary avenues to knowledge. To live with books and be ignorant of nature, of the facts and laws in the midst of which God has placed our lives, was to Froebel no less senseless and irreligious.

He taught no catechism to little children, but he would have them learn to worship God through nature, to love Him as the

Father of whose love and government their earthly parents present the intelligible type. The key-note of Froebel's system may be said to be that we live and move and have our being in God, whose visible manifestation is the universe on which He has impressed His laws, which He has endowed us with faculties to decipher and obey. Thus to Him we are responsible that the children He has trusted to our care shall be trained into fitness so to obey and understand His will. It is, as serving religion, no less than as developing the creative faculty, that Froebel lays great stress on the cultivation of the imagination, which is so deadened by ordinary teaching. He felt how much we need to kindle early that sacred spark which illumines life with beauty, which lights the flame on every altar where man sacrifices his baser instincts to lofty ideals—gain to patriotism—self to humanity —the world to God. The child in whom a soul has thus been awakened brings to the dull routine of school an impulse that will give life to that routine itself. It will take years of bad teaching and bad management to make such a child lose the feeling that his life is something beyond school lessons or school play, that it is in what he *does* and in what he *loves*.

The one real difficulty to overcome with Kinder-Garten children is that of passing from object-lessons to book-lessons; but if this transition be made under the guidance of Kinder-Garten teachers, it is accomplished without trouble or annoyance to the little ones. In the preparatory or *transition class*, as it is usually called, in which this change is effected, the children learn to read and write and to work sums with figures, and thus when they go to school at eight years old they know all that is expected at that age, and much besides that others do not know.

Nothing illustrates the benefit of the early development of intelligence in the children, while all their lessons have been play, than the facility with which this work of the transition classes is effected. A child's difficulty in learning to read is that he has no skill in perceiving the different forms of letters, and no habit of attaching one correct name to the form he recognizes—his eye and ear are equally unexercised; but the child trained in the Kinder-Garten has exercised both in a great variety of ways, and he distinguishes the forms of the letters very rapidly. So with writing, we have first that same difficulty of seeing correctly, and the next great difficulty of the unpractised hand, at once feeble and clumsy, that cannot trace the given line even when the child has been brought to see its form and direction. Now in the Kinder-Garten the little hands have been daily exercised, not only in drawing lines in various directions, but in delicate and accurate work. The children have learned to perceive when they have worked correctly, or incorrectly; thus writing becomes a comparatively easy application of an art already acquired. As regards such arithmetic as children are expected to learn at that age, the only difficulty for the Kinder-Garten pupil will be the method of working a simple sum on the slate; he is used to deal with numbers, both with units and fractions, and he is quite familiar in a practical way with some elementary notions of geometry. He has also been interested with stories from history, and he knows something of that foundation of physical geography that may be made so interesting to children, that may be taught practically in a field or by a roadside, or in a class-room, wherever we can find or make inequalities of soil, and show how water runs in one direction instead of another. As regards elementary knowledge, then, he will be quite on a par with other children, and, owing to the method pursued, he will possess it better. Thus we may be sure that as soon as the mechanical difficulties of reading are overcome he will at once read intelligently, because he will feel an interest in what he can understand, and will know when he does *not* understand; and his wish to learn more will spring from recollections of the pleasure he has had in learning hitherto.

I have said what are the leading characteristics of Froebel's system, and it follows from thence that it is mainly distinguished from ordinary school teaching by making the knowledge of ideas wait upon the knowledge of facts, and by making the cultivation of the memory subordinate to the development of the faculties of observation and reasoning, and of the active tendencies of the child, both physical and mental. This mental discipline is, of course, part of the purpose of all school teaching; but Froebel learnt by his own experience as a schoolmaster, and we may see it verified every day, that the press of matter to be taught leaves scanty time for this gradual development of human faculty, even if at school age many a wrong habit and bias had not already been given. Thus to rescue early childhood from such errors and to guide the development aright from the first, was, he felt, the only means by which we might ensure that after school-work should bear its proper fruit. If we doubt the need of such preparation let us consider for a moment what is the ordinary condition of a child going to school at eight or nine years old.

It naturally differs very much in different classes of society. In the upper ranks, where mothers have leisure, and *ought* to have cultivation—where attendance is abundant, and *may* be good, children ought to come well prepared with the elements of such knowledge as the school demands—reading, writing, some arithmetic, and perhaps a little geography and English history. In the working classes, where children go through the infant school, they also come in some measure prepared, they have learnt order and obedience, which too many careful homes neglect to teach. But between these two extremes we have the large middle class, through its great variety of degrees, in which mothers are more or less occupied, where servants of an inferior kind are employed, and where generally, at least, the most that can be done is to keep children out of positive mischief. In what state of forwardness children from such homes come to school, not merely at eight years old but at ten, or for girls even at twelve and fourteen, let those who are practically engaged in school-work declare. But if these children had spent four or five years in the Kinder-Garten and the transition class, they would not only bring, as we have seen above, those elements of knowledge that are required, but have learnt in some degree *how to learn*, and in the measure of their progress *have nothing to unlearn*. Let those who labour day by day with inert minds, never yet awakened to a wish for knowledge, or a sense of beauty, or a feeling of pleasure in mental activity, tell us how much valuable school time they would save if the raw material were thus prepared to their hand. And this element of time is one that must seriously be taken into consideration with schools of every grade. This. it is that cramps the best teacher's efforts and grinds down admirable theories of education to indifferent schemes of instruction.

It seems a long time from seven to seventeen, but modern life demands much, and its demands force the work of instruction into grooves it is difficult to abandon. The University, or professional exigencies, govern schools. Upper schools govern both the lower and the preparatory; and thus each step prepares for a higher step of knowledge, and the only thing that is not prepared for is life itself, making its thousand calls upon will and character which we have allowed chance influences to form; life which calls for all active energies, and of which, as Matthew Arnold so truly says, "Conduct makes up three parts, and knowledge only one." And the intellectual qualities that affect conduct, judgment, accuracy—that power of reasoning promptly and correctly concerning things we habitually deal with, which we call common sense,—these are the direct fruits, not of varied knowledge but of the mental discipline which should accompany the acquisition of knowledge. Unfortunately, the pressure of the modern demand for knowledge and instruction overpowers education, and will continue to do so, unless we can counteract this deteriorating influence by using for true educational purposes those early years that are free from outer claims; thus making the child by the time he goes to school amenable to the higher discipline of good teaching.

But hitherto we have considered the case of children of the upper and middle classes only: it is time to turn to the children of the poor, for whom every motive that makes Kinder-Garten training a valuable preparation for schools is strengthened tenfold. The boy who is to go through a great public school to the University sorely needs time, as we have seen above, to acquire the indispensable amount of instruction without neglecting education; but he has a grand life before him if he knows how to use it—leisure—means of knowledge, stimulants to ambition which might almost suffice alone to rescue men from selfish sloth; he has time, if he learn how to use it, to repair the omissions of the past, as far as the laws of nature will ever allow the past to be repaired. Others, again, who go through our grammar and middle-class schools into the world of commonplace business will find in a life of increasing labour a remedy at least to the mental inertness that follows ordinary school teaching. They also have opportunities of knowledge—a variety of interests that may serve to keep the soul alive amid the deadening influence of ceaseless money-making labour; but when we look to the children of the poor we know that their school life is their all of education, except such as life itself gives to every human being according to the influences domestic, social, or political under which he lives, and that this practical education for them can scarcely be an elevating one. What we have then to do is, in those scanty years that poverty can grant to school discipline, to make that discipline such that the child shall be fit to learn the lesson of life in a right spirit. Instruction gives him possession of the most indispensable keys to knowledge—it is hard enough often to do that; but education of a higher order will alone give him the wish to use those keys, and teach him to feel that he cannot live upon bread alone, however large a portion of his existence must be given merely to providing the bread. Intellectual life is a barren desert to the child who leaves school with such knowledge as an elementary school can have taught under the given conditions, and whose intelligence has received no other training than such teaching can afford. There is barely time for what is imperatively laid down; how can the schoolmaster mould the dull, ill-trained children that come to him full of false ideas and wrong habits, into thinking, observing human beings, able to work and to think intelligently and accurately? And yet if he has not done that, what have these schools done for the nation that pays for them? There is in the rudiments of knowledge no talisman for making good citizens; and though no one more fully appreciates than I do all that school does for children, of that class especially, independently of instruction, yet I say if we cannot supplement the instruction with such mental discipline as shall teach them how to use the knowledge, and create a desire to do so, then we are not educating the people. Nor am I alluding here to the desire to use knowledge which springs from the wish to rise in the world—that motive is put forward too often and too strongly to need any help of mine—rather would I see it less powerful; what I mean by using the knowledge acquired at school, is that use whereby life is made a better and nobler thing, whereby the face of the earth is beautified through all we know of the many forms of life that speak of God and His laws all around us, whereby a man does whatever he has to do more intelligently, and fulfils every duty with a better understanding. It is this influence of such poor culture as we can give which alone can entitle us to say that our schools are educating another generation to do good service to the nation, and how, I ask again, can time be found for such careful mental discipline added to the hard labour of teaching? But if Froebel's system prevailed in our infant schools, then we might hope that school teaching beginning upon such a foundation of mental discipline as that system affords, and with the help of the progress already made in certain branches of instruction—the years from seven to eleven or twelve would produce fruits which at present the most zealous master or mistress cannot dare to hope for. And if the children through stress of poverty leave school very early, they will yet take with them some ineffaceable good. It is easy to forget reading and writing through years of disuse, it is not easy to forget the use of our eyes when we have learnt to take pleasure in observing, nor the habit of judging, of reasoning upon what comes before us, when once the mind has been stirred to take pleasure in the exercise. It must be remembered that the development of moral and intellectual faculties is as natural, as much a part of the laws of our being, as physical development, the only difference being that it carries with it conscious action, and therefore the possibility of being mentally influenced for good or evil; thus the degree of such development that the child has attained under our guidance at a certain age has a far more permanent character than the degree of his knowledge. The latter is given from without, the former is his own growth, an intrinsic part henceforth of his being, and therefore it is that I say the child trained in the Kinder-Garten will keep what he has gained, while the mere school-taught child may lose all he has painfully acquired before he reaches manhood.

Differences of knowledge must exist between different classes of men, like differences of material means, the one in a great measure owing to the other. The poor cannot be said to be disinherited of wealth, because wealth is not a natural possession, nor one that ever can belong to all. But those are indeed the disinherited of the earth who are deprived of what nature designed for them, whose true human capacity has not been unfolded. The poor man suffers *privation* from deficient knowledge as from deficient comfort; but he suffers *wrong* when his education is so defective that he cannot use his human faculties aright, when his senses are blunted, his observation and judgment insecure—his moral sense and activity uncultivated. And it is this disinheriting of our poorer brethren that we may avoid by an early methodical training such as Froebel has taught us.

We owe, then, no small debt of gratitude to the London School Board for their effort to try this great experiment, and I trust that Sir Charles Reed, who has so kindly consented to take the chair this evening, will tell us something of his views of the subject and the prospect of success he sees before him. Full success can be expected only when all infant school mistresses are duly trained for Kinder-Garten work. They may then be trusted to introduce such modifications as the large numbers in our infant schools may render necessary.

I ought, I fear, to apologize for the length of time I have detained you; yet I must touch upon one other point, which I consider of the highest importance, and this is the advantage of Froebel's system to all that portion of our population who are engaged in industrial pursuits. When boys or girls leave school to be apprenticed to some trade they go to their new work with hands and eyes absolutely uncultivated; the girls have, perhaps, done some needlework, and are so far in a better condition than the boys; the occupation of the latter since leaving school has probably been of the roughest description, or has not required any peculiar manipulation—as in the case of messengers, etc. When, therefore, they come to learn a trade they begin with clumsy fingers, with that *untrue habit of vision*, if I may so express myself, which belongs to those who have never learned the difference between accurate and inaccurate impressions, and all these preliminary disadvantages have to be got over before the smallest progress can be made in the technical part of whatever new work they have to learn. Now if we suppose these children to have been first trained in the Kinder-Garten, taught there to observe resemblances and differences of forms and colours, and directions of lines, to reproduce accurately what they have observed accurately, to have acquired a certain sureness and delicacy of handling, which would be further cultivated by drawing at school—then these boys and girls would enter any industrial apprenticeship or any technical school in a very different condition. They would be at once able to grapple with ordinary difficulties instead of beginning the education of their hands and senses, and would in consequence reach much sooner the degree of proficiency that ensures payment for work. The moment of beginning to receive wages would be hastened in proportion to the time saved from that preliminary preparation which is in fact not technical learning at all, but part of the indispensable training of the human being apart from any peculiar purpose. When mental discipline generally is neglected in childhood it is with some tacit assumption that school studies will supply it; but this combined mental and physical training we generally ignore altogether. Yet when we withhold that cultivation of the senses and of manual dexterity we are not merely heaping difficulties in the way of a few who must later acquire what we do not teach them early, but we maim children generally in the use of some of the most important faculties, we rob them of what nature designed for them, we venture to choose what part of their natural gifts it suits us to put them in possession of; in their helpless ignorance we have not honestly done our part as guardians, for we have buried in a napkin the talents for which they will have to render account. We might find instances to illustrate the loss so incurred in every department of industrial and art labour, just as we might have traced in a variety of directions what I have barely indicated of the loss so incurred by children of the leisure classes; but it is impossible in one lecture to treat so large a subject in anything but the most cursory manner, and I can only hope that I have said enough to establish my main proposition, that the Kinder-Garten is the right and true vestibule of the school, that it prepares the child for all it is to learn there, and provides the groundwork for the full cultivation and discipline of all the faculties which school as at present constituted, having to labour against the neglected condition of the children who enter, cannot have time to undertake.

Education, which is the preparation for life, must be one in purpose and in spirit throughout all its phases. Froebel built altogether upon this truth, and therefore begins from the first what each successive step is to unfold and strengthen. When, therefore, we ask if the Kinder-Garten affects school life—if it furthers its work, it is questioning whether Froebel did or did not adjust the means to the end, whether his method is education at all, or only a way of amusing and exercising little children. If the latter only, it may have an importance of its own, but not the importance we claim for it. Now if we once admit its true human purpose as far as it goes, if we acknowledge that the faculties whose dawning power he watches and draws out, are the same faculties which in their ripe vigour the philosopher, the poet, the statesman, use for the benefit of mankind; if the will and character he teaches us to discipline in the nursery are acknowledged to be germs of the same powers that make useful citizens, social benefactors, the leaders and heroes of our race, then school years, which are only one stage of that unbroken process of effort and discipline, which we call life, cannot stand isolated. Those who rule them cannot neglect or ignore what has gone before any more than they can be indifferent to the claims of the years that are to follow. Shakespeare says of man that " He looks before and after," and this is more specially true of the educator than of any other human being save the statesman.

THE KINDER-GARTEN

IN RELATION TO FAMILY LIFE.

By Emily Shirreff.

THE last time I had the pleasure of addressing you, my theme was the Kinder-Garten in relation to schools; to-night I move a stage further back in the consideration of the system, and wish to dwell on the Kinder-Garten in relation to family life. The other was most important to be brought forward, to be pressed forward even, in the interest of our outward work. The Kinder-Garden, as I have said, will not be valued, its peculiar mode of training will not be estimated properly in the scholastic profession till men have realized what benefit scholars will derive from their pupils being prepared for them in the Kinder-Garten. But our subject to-day is a wider and more important one still. School is but an episode of life, Home is the centre, the pivot of life itself. That nation is at a great disadvantage that has not good schools, but that nation is poor to the roots that has not a healthy home life. When, therefore, we speak of a thing as true and good—of such things, I mean, as affect the conduct of life—it is well to see what relation it bears to the holiest portion of life—that of the family. There virtue or vice, strength or weakness, duty or self-indulgence, love or selfishness, must do their fullest work; there human life may be made most wretched, or may be blessed as though a ray of Heaven's own light shone upon its homeliest details. Into this life, under one or other of its manifold forms, each human being is born, and here all that is good or all that is bad around him, must necessarily begin his education years before that of school begins. Our business to-night is to inquire what Fröbel's system can do to help the good, to avert the evil, to direct the strong impulses which parental love creates but cannot enlighten. The first effect of its influence is to raise our estimate of the early helpless years of human life, to make us see in them not a mere period of physical growth, but the seed-time of all that cultivation and discipline may bring to a rich harvest in after years.

In ordinary apprehension education is associated with lessons; even in well kept nurseries, where a most valuable education is actually begun, it is not called by that name, it is not considered as simply the beginning of the same work that will be continued through childhood and youth, and therefore no method rules it, no distinct purpose is kept in view. Were it once so considered it would rise in importance, it would no longer be left to nurses, but would become the mother's first care, it would no longer be left to mothers alone, but would grow in importance with fathers also. They have been accustomed when they thought of the education of their children to look forward to a more or less distant time, to consider the school they would choose, the subjects—classical or modern— they would have them instructed in, &c.; but of that first growth of habits and associations, of notions and capabilities which springs up in the early home years, and will be carried by the child to school, to affect his whole career there, the father has seldom thought at all, and this is what acquaintance with Fröbel's system will make him think of; one of the greatest benefits that system can confer upon us is this, of turning the serious attention of parents to the importance of that early training, and through it to a new sense of their own responsibility, since with them alone it must rest. The evil that I pointed out in speaking of the relation of the Kinder-Garten to schools is the evil of instructing children instead of drawing out their faculties, of dealing with abstractions, while the interest of the young mind can only be awakened by external objects; the evil that is laid bare, as we consider the Kinder-Garten in relation to family life, is the neglect of early training owing to ignorance on the part of parents. In the case of schools, therefore, we hope the Fröbel system will lead the way to a vast reform in our methods of education; in the case of home life we trust that it will awaken women to a true sense of their most important duty, that it will make them realize that, for good or for ill, and consciously or unconsciously, every mother necessarily educates her child from the first hour of dawning intelligence, and that while other teachers have simply made choice of a vocation, they have no choice left, but are educators by right divine. There perhaps never was a time when children held so large a place in home life as they do now, and the sense of responsibility for their welfare, mental and physical, is gravely acknowledged; but women have not yet realized that the right care for that welfare needs knowledge as well as love, and this is what the influence of Fröbel's system will bring home to them.

Let us now inquire what is the position of the Kinder-Garten among us at the present time, before we consider what it may become, and what influence it may exercise. It is making way undoubtedly, and has some true and ardent supporters; but it has many supporters for the sake of novelty. Fashion is even beginning to set in the same direction, and curiosity has been keenly excited in many places. But among all who visit it, of those who even send their children to it, how many, apart from the few mentioned above, take it *au serieux*, and not as a mere harmless way of keeping children quiet and amused, one expedient among many for evading the necessity of discipline before schooltime? This frivolous view of the Kinder-Garten is one of the greatest obstacles our teachers now have to encounter; the effects are everywhere visible; classes are opened, competent teaching provided, and a fair number of children gathered together, but the following week perhaps half those children are kept away, and the classes necessarily thrown into confusion; sometimes the treachery of our climate is really to blame; but more often, I believe, it is mere fancy, mere ignorance that it is a thing of real importance that they are playing with; for, after all, in spite of the climate, there is no country in which children take such regular out-of-door exercise as in England, and if they can walk out at all, they might walk to the Kinder-Garten, and there they would get a great deal of healthy exercise without exposure to the weather, so that in truth there is less danger for children who spend the morning there than for those who depend for all their exercise on the daily walks. Another common obstacle I believe to be the jealousy of nurses. They do not like such a rival to their authority or to their affection. These women are as ignorant as the cottagers' wives, but far more mischievous, for the poor woman labouring for her family is glad of the relief of getting her children cared for, while the nurse only feels the loss of power and possibly of affection. In other ways the right influence of the Kinder-Garten may often be more thwarted among the rich than among the poor. The latter may by their ways and their ignorance unconsciously oppose the influence of school; but they are generally impressed with the vast superiority of school teaching to any they could give, and they do not *consciously* oppose it; but with the upper classes this is quite different; if parents do not go entirely with the school, they express their different opinion, and display their indifference. Servants take the cue from them, and set up a jealous antagonism to the schoolroom authority. Thus the child's reverence for the instruction he receives is lessened, and the very fact of his realizing a divided opinion among those whom he ought to revere is so far destructive of the educational value of the training. It is, then, in some important respects most difficult to establish the system in rich homes with nursery establishments where, unless the mother gives the right tone, the prevailing influence round the child is a disastrous combination of luxury and ignorance. It is there that caprice is most likely to reign, it is there that children are supposed often to need change of air, to be wanted for some visit, to be so loaded with toys and books, and surrounded with slaves to their pleasures, that the simple toys and amusements of the Kinder-Garten have less charm ; also, I am sorry to say, it is from such homes that children come occasionally to the Kinder-Garten with a degree of ill-breeding that speaks of a very low moral tone when at home ; children who are not only rebellious against authority, but haughty and insolent to their companions, and even to their teachers. What education is going on in homes where such things are possible, and what is to become of children whose mothers are to such a degree ignorant of education?

With regard to lower social classes, we have already pointed out one advantage possessed by the children of the poor; another is that they are obliged to attend school, and thus whenever the schools are good they are brought early under more promising educational conditions than those of their richer neighbours, unless among the latter the mothers are fit for their task. The Kinder-Garten will, as I have had occasion more than once to point out, open to them a prospect of improvement that is undreamed of now, by adding the cultivation of their faculties of mind and sense to the instruction they now receive. In this class the Kinder-Garten will gradually exercise remarkable influence over family life, for when girls have been educated themselves in that system, and especially if the time should come that I am so anxious to see, when every girl before leaving school is made to pass a certain time as a student-teacher in the Kinder-Garten department, every house in the country will receive the seeds of educational principles, the wife of the labourer no less than the peeress will understand God's command to her when He grants her the joy and privilege of motherhood, she will know that she has yet another duty to perform for her child beside the physical care which had seemed before to be the utmost she could compass. She may possess little knowledge or time to do much herself, but she will refrain from doing mischief, and will feel increased confidence in placing her child in better instructed hands. Again, the instruction given to the eldest child will fit the mother herself to do more for the next. Her own experience will be supplemented by what she has seen the elder gain from the greater knowledge and experience that have directed his training.

But between the artizan's or labourer's home, where the temptation is neglect through ignorance, and the wealthy homes where the danger is corruption through luxury and servility, we have to consider the vast middle class in its innumerable gradations. There we find the most varied forms of family life, and in all, the admittance of Fröbel's system would bring improvement, while in all some peculiar circumstances present more or less obstacles to its admittance.

In many the mother does the whole or nearly the whole of the house-work, and is more burdened than the labourer's wife, because she has to provide for the claims of gentility as well as for the more positive needs of life. She is too ignorant to care for the training of the Kinder-Garten, and cannot be troubled to take her children there. In many others the struggle is to have a little money over at the end of the year, since expense must be met for elder children, or for healthy excursions, &c., so the expense of teaching babies, who might be crawling or toddling about the floor for another year or two, seems foolish extravagance. This form of objection is the most general, and in various degrees it prompts all the discontent about school fees, and the too common neglect of girls' education, because it can be neglected without apparent loss, while the boys cannot hope for employment unless they reach a given standard of instruction. There is too often truth—painful truth—in the objection, many a family can meet the expense of education only by a real sacrifice; but the feeling that is now growing that such sacrifice must be made if the worldly prospects of boys are not to be destroyed, will receive altogether fresh intensity and be extended to both sexes whenever the spread of Fröbel's principles shall have convinced parents that not instruction but education, training of the entire capabilities of the human creature, is the debt they owe to each child. Then mothers will study education, and the fathers will feel the importance of providing the means for it.

Two of the greatest obstacles the Kinder-Garten has daily to encounter are—1st, the late age at which the children are sent; 2nd, the monomania of parents with regard to reading and writing; both these show ignorance of the right principle of education, and both would disappear if Fröbel's views of infant training were accepted. The expression, a late age, as applied to the children of six years old, sounds, perhaps, rather strange; one might imagine a good deal of laughing at it; but it is correct, nevertheless, as applied to Kinder-Garten pupils. In Fröbel's system the instruction, occupations, and games are all addressed to minds that have not been previously instructed in any other manner; they aim at giving, in one sense, first impressions, the first that are purposely directed to fix attention and provoke an exercise of reasoning, and they are carefully graduated; each links on to the other, leading the infant intelligence a little further at each step, but ever in the same direction, and with constant care not to break the sequence or scatter the attention. The whole intention of this infant training is to form habits and associations—moral, intellectual, and physical—at a time when there is nothing to hinder the direction we wish to give. Now, if children of six years old are sent into a Kinder-Garten, they come with their own stock of previously acquired notions and habits, and we have to undo as well as to train, and run the great risk of mischief to the younger children. Children of six know, or think they know, many of the things that their younger companions are learning; but they have learned them differently, without order or system, without the links that in Fröbel's system connect the knowledge and the skill acquired with the knowledge that is to come next in orderly sequence. If, then, parents have kept their children in the ordinary way till six years old, they had better do their best with them still in the same way, and not send them to get confused notions of a better system and help to confuse others. In many cases children are sent because mothers think it very likely in some way to be a good thing for children who are getting beyond nursery management and are too young for school; they will be kept in order for some hours of the day, and perhaps they will learn something—at any rate they are safe, and the nurses or mothers have more time for other work. It is hardly necessary to remark that when Fröbel's system shall have been studied widely, and that parents know *why* the Kinder-Garten occupations and games may be expected to produce a good result, all such capricious playing with them will be at an end; the parents will have educated themselves into a comprehension of the value of educational principles in dealing with their children.

The other obstacle I have mentioned—the monomania about reading and writing—has partly the same origin. There is the same desire to teach the children something that will keep them quiet, and lead to their amusing themselves without trouble to their elders; and there is that same profound ignorance of educational principles that leads parents to believe that teaching to read is education. Doubtless, besides being the most important instrument for acquiring knowledge, it can also be made an instrument of mental training in the hands of an educator; but in how many homes can this be said to be the case? What more mechanical than the ordinary teaching to read and to write, and what less educational than the heaping of story-books round a child to let him amuse himself, that is, to pick up wrong notions, because he only half understands what he reads, to use words that convey no meaning, and adopt sentiments without a perception of what they imply.

The mother's hurry to teach her children to read is often based on this wish to keep them quiet and amused, and often also on the feeling that her children must not lag behind other children; she would have a sense of shame if Jane or Harry next door could read to themselves while her own Jack or Mary were unable to do so. The father's impatience is generally of a different kind; he knows that schools grow more and more exacting, that there is in this uncomfortable phase of the world's history a larger and larger quantity of knowledge to be acquired, and he cannot separate knowledge from books, nor the power of acquiring it from reading and writing. One father I have heard of who avows that he can take no interest in his boys till they begin the Latin grammar —where the limit of his interest in his girls, if he has any, may be placed, I do not know. If there be anything that the girls get rid of as rapidly after they leave school as boys shuffle off the Latin on which eight years of life have been mainly spent, perhaps this father would take his stand there. He worships a school fetish, and with that we cannot meddle.

Now, if we could once get Fröbel's system widely known, if the notion that the training and discipline of every human faculty from the earliest dawn of intelligence is the education that must underlie all other education, if this notion, I repeat, could be received, all this would be at an end. Reading and writing, to say nothing of Latin grammar, would be reduced to their proper level as instruments of instruction, to be used when the mental and bodily faculties are so developed that they can be used with advantage. If parents who suffer under this mania for early reading could be persuaded to postpone the comparison of their children's acquirements with those of other children for two years or so, and let those two years be spent in our transition classes, we might perhaps make ready converts. It is quite right that care should be taken that children do not go to school unfit to take their place in class with those of the same ages; let us then consider what a child going to school at nine years old can fairly be expected to know—reading, writing, spelling, a little French or Latin, as the case may be, the four rules of arithmetic, some notion of Scripture history and geography, and the same with respect to our own country. If a child goes to school at nine, knowing these things accurately, we may, I think, safely affirm that he or she will be well placed in the school, and keep that place. Now, any Kinder-Garten teacher will surely promise that a child who has been kept strictly to Kinder-Garten work even till seven years old, and then passed on to the transition classes, will in two years attain such a degree of forwardness in school learning, without the least pressure or difficulty. If we look closer at the work of those two years, we shall see how this is effected. Writing is singularly easy to him; of geography he has learnt something, and in a thorough manner; the working of figures is new, but arithmetic far beyond what is required is familiar to the child; and though reading is a novel and difficult art, the Kinder-Garten exercises have given facility and accuracy in tracing resemblances and differences, and in recognising forms; the child's memory is so trained to this, that letters and combinations of letters will quickly be discerned and remembered. Also we must remember that if he did not learn to read in the Kinder-Garten, he learnt to speak distinctly, and to use accurate and well articulated words. He has a larger vocabulary than other children, because his attention has been turned to more things. Thus the actual school learning required by the age of nine will be of easy acquirement; but in addition to this, he will have gained many things that enter into no school time-table, and it is to this that it must be our business to turn the attention of parents. We must make it evident to them what their children have gained in general development of mental and physical capacity. The latter will be shown in suppleness and dexterity of limb, in delicacy and accuracy of eye and hand, the mental growth will be manifested by quickness and accuracy of observation, by clearness of apprehension, leaving no doubt whether a thing is understood or not; by the development of active creative powers, for Kinder-Garten pupils can *do* as well as understand; by interest in what has been learnt, because the mind has never been wearied with uninteresting matter, has never wandered in the dreary fog of half comprehension; by some power of reasoning, accurately on the objects brought under consideration, the why, whence, and how of such things having habitually roused the children's attention. It will be shown by a sense of beauty and symmetry in form, by a readiness to apprehend certain elementary truths of geometry which in the concrete have been familiar; the moral benefit also will have been considerable. Little children learn much by living with their equals, the gentleness, the habit of working together, and sharing a common interest, the affection they learn to feel towards their teachers, the reverence kept up by remaining always under the rule of their superiors, and not under servants, and the cultivation, through contemplation of nature, and of human goodness in many forms, of that deeply rooted religious sentiment in the child's nature which rises to the notion of God, by realizing the wisdom and goodness of parental love. All this adds to the moral influence of home, and thus reacts upon it. In a word, the parents will not fail to recognize that their children, besides the little bundle of knowledge required for entrance upon school life, will carry these minds and bodies trained to enlarge their small possessions in every direction. And if parents do realise this fact, then the Kinder-Garten has educated them, as well as their children; in one important particular, it will have made them see the difference between the instruction they might have given in the common way with books alone, and the education that has been given by drawing out the children's own faculties within the circle of visible objects That circle comprises largely natural phenomena, which most children are eager to know about, but concerning which they seldom get the answer they require. Natural History, birds, beasts, and flowers, the commonest facts of general physics, the changes of seasons, the sun, moon, and stars, these excite the curiosity of all but the dullest children; but how many of those who are around them in general can direct and stimulate that curiosity in the right direction. How many, in speaking of some particular object, can draw it even in outline, or, if it be a plant, give it its right name? But if once the value of Kinder-Garten training can be made apparent, surely no intelligent mother—from the so-called educated classes—will allow herself to remain dumb and helpless before her child, from ignorance of the facts that he learns from the Kinder-Garten teachers. The mother cannot expect to keep always on a level with the advanced instruction given to her sons or daughters, but surely she could not bear to think that she was unfit to satisfy the desire for knowledge of her little child, when once she has satisfied herself that such knowledge is good for the child. She would not choose to be so out of sympathy with the creature round which all her heart-strings twine, as not be able to enter into every phase his unfolding intelligence is going through. Ignorance, however, in matters such as these is harmless as compared to that of principles of education, of the knowledge which enables us to watch and aid the development of childish faculty, to guard mental and physical health; and this it is which the influence of Fröbel's system with the weight it lays upon infant training will force upon the attention of mothers. On the importance of early impressions the scientific fatalist and the earnest Christian like Fröbel take their stand together. Both agree that the surroundings of the child from the first are what impress the pliable nature and form associations that affect the whole development. Yet the mother, who would give her life to make her child's life happy, remains ignorant. But when once Kinder-Garten principles are generally accepted, young mothers will feel that so large a task must require preparation, that to learn the A, B, C of work to be performed at the moment the work is pressing is not the act of a reasonable being; thus the principle that education begins with the dawn of life will lead to a preparatory study of education, and will in time lead to the acceptance of this important doctrine that no woman's own education is complete without a study of education; she may be accomplished in many ways, or may even have reached high attainments, but she is not trained for life which is the real office of education, unless she has studied how to acquit herself in that most important position that life can possibly open to her. I think I may say that my experience as a single woman has not been different from that of most others, yet I have more than once had the care of childern thrown upon me, and I believe the exceptions are rare where women are not called upon more or less to deal with children, and I long for the time when it shall be deemed as unseemly for a woman not to understand their proper management as it is for a man to be unfit to do active service in defence of his hearth and country. The service in each case is pointed out by Nature, and the man or woman is a recreant to the highest social duty who is unfit to perform it.

The principal means therefore by which the influence of the Kinder-Gartens will work a reform in family life will be by raising in their own eyes, and in that of men, the estimate of woman's natural position, and of the tone of character and culture that are indispensable to her fulfilling the mission worthily. A slighting view of early education naturally detracts from the respect due to that mission, and feeds that most mischievous of all ignorant delusions, the notion that simply because a woman is a mother, she is fit to fulfil her duty to her children.

It is easy to believe that little is needed to enable any woman to educate very little children, so long as education means only putting words into a child's mouth, or even maintaining such moral discipline as, thank God, is cared for in most English homes; but this same charge is seen to be far from easy, when education is held to mean the careful watching that tends, but never thwarts, the unfolding of the child's own nature; that studies the first symptoms of character, of peculiarities in the mental as well as the physical organization; that allows no neglect of the bodily for the mental growth and welfare, nor of the latter for the former; but keeps all in harmonious order, respecting the entire freedom of individual development, while guiding it so step by step that as the bodily organs strengthen, the mental growth shall correspond; that what the eyes behold shall excite first pleasure, then curiosity, then attention, then observation and memory of what has been observed; till the child is led to discover for himself one after another some wonders of the marvellous world upon which his senses have just opened. All these faculties will be active, no doubt, without our care, but their exercise will tend to no given purpose, there will be no method, and therefore no orderly advance, and no preparation for future progress. So also with the active instincts of children. The little things will play, with or without our help; but we learn nothing, and can teach nothing from their play, if we do not carefully watch it as the manifestation of natural aptitudes and desires, that we have to train for higher uses. These are some of the educational points to which Fröbel directs attention, and the Kinder-Garten games and occupations—the practical system in which these principles are embodied—afford at once a study and a guide to those who are concerned in education. When, therefore, mothers become familiar with that system they will be able to test their own capability for the office, which, under any circumstances, they cannot give up. The Kinder-Garten, which we hear accused of taking children out of home, robbing the mothers of their right and privilege, &c.—the Kinder-Garten can perform but half its work, can at best take hold of the child partially and imperfectly, unless rounded and supplemented by home education. Instead of displacing the mother, it makes the imperative necessity of her care more apparent. And for this reason it is that the appeal to mothers from a Fröbel society is so urgent. It is a question of all but life or death to the system we hold to be so valuable.

The extreme difficulty we find in attracting students for Kinder-Garten training arises partly, no doubt, from the long prevailing English prejudice against training teachers, but still more from that same ignorance of the importance of early education that I have already deplored. Any one has been thought sufficiently instructed to teach little children; the thing that seemed so easy was trusted to ignorant hands, and this whole department has fallen into contempt. When, therefore, young women are told that two years of serious study are required to prepare for our Kinder-Garten examinations, they naturally turn back surprised and disappointed. This will all be changed when women generally take a higher view of their natural position; then it will be felt that no labour is too great for those who are to undertake its duties, and that if women had no other object in view to make them desire culture of the noblest kind, they would have it in the first great duty of training themselves to be educators of the next generation. With the increased sense of the value of infant education, there must arise an increased value for the influence and the education of women. The former would be seen to extend over the most important field of human interest; the latter could no longer be a matter of indifference —of *passe temps*—of preparation for mere success, whether in drawing-rooms or in the labour-market; it would have a serious and a lofty purpose, apart from ambitions great or small—it would consecrate, once and for all, the power of women to the highest service of the nation. Fröbel appealed solemnly to women to enter upon this high form of service; and if his system, as it takes its place among us, tends to hasten such a reform, we may surely say, that great and beneficial as the influence of the Kinder-Garten is in relation to schools, it will be in relation to family life deeper and more far-reaching still.

Finally, what can we as members of the Fröbel Society do towards promoting this reform? Those among us who are teachers have this very clear before them. The more strictly they adhere to principles in their course, the more they bring them forward and banish mere mechanical teaching, the more they will force parents to see that this is no nursery amusement, but education as earnest and thorough as any given by school or university; and we who are not teachers, can aid in the missionary work that belongs to all pioneers of reform. We can each within our own circle strive to make the new education known, can take care to put it on the true grounds, to show where it differs from education addressed to the memory; we can try to bring young girls to learn and to help in Kinder-Garten teaching; we can also do good by trying to extend a plan I heard of with great pleasure the other day, that of mothers taking it by turns to attend the classes with their children, bringing a number of different minds to imbibe the spirit of the system which will lead to a certain number resolving to study it thoroughly, while others will do so partially for some practical purpose at the moment, but none, we may safely affirm, will remain indifferent. And thus here a little and there a little, by slow and often halting steps, our small society will become one of the most powerful instruments of a reform, which, beginning at the core of national life, will gradually affect the most powerful currents of national thought and feeling.

www.ingramcontent.com/pod-product-compliance
Lightning Source LLC
Chambersburg PA
CBHW030353170426
43202CB00010B/1356